CONTENTS

MAP OF EUROPE SINCE 1992

Note: In order to simplify the use of this book, all names, locations and geographic designations are as provided in *The Times World Atlas*, or other traditionally accepted major sources of reference, as of the time of described events.

Helion & Company Limited
Unit 8 Amherst Business Centre
Budbrooke Road
Warwick
CV34 5WE
England
Tel. 01926 499 619
Email: info@helion.co.uk
Website: www.helion.co.uk
Twitter: @helionbooks
https://helionbooks.wordpress.com/

Colour Profiles: David Bocquelet

Cover image: *Pion* of the 43rd 'Taras Triasylo' Artillery Brigade. (43 Art.)

Designed and typeset by Mach 3 Solutions (www.mach3solutions.co.uk)
Cover design Paul Hewitt, Battlefield Design (www.battlefield-design.co.uk)

ISBN: 978-1-804517-21-5

British Library Cataloguing-in-Publication Data
A catalogue record for this book is available from the British Library

We always welcome receiving book proposals from prospective authors.

ABBREVIATIONS AND ACRONYMS

AAMG	anti-aircraft machine gun
ACRV	artillery command & reconnaissance vehicle
AFV	armoured fighting vehicle
AP	armour-piercing
APC	armoured personnel carrier
APU	auxiliary power unit
ARVGK	*Artilleriya rezerva Verkhovnogo Glavnokomandovaniya* (Supreme High Command artillery reserve)
AT	anti-tank
ATGM	anti-tank guided missile
BB	base bleed
BMS	battlefield management system
C2	command & control
DPICM	dual-purpose improved conventional munition
DPRK	Democratic People's Republic of Korea, colloquially North Korea
FCS	fire control system
GPS	Global Positioning System
GBTU	*Glavnoe bronetankovoe upravlenie* (Main AFV Directorate)
GRAU	*Glavnoe raketno-artilleriyskoe upravlenie* (Main Rocket & Artillery Directorate)
HEAT	high explosive, anti-tank
HE-Frag	high explosive, fragmentation; used interchangeably with 'HE'
IFV	infantry fighting vehicle
INS	inertial navigation systems
KB	*konstruktorskoye byuro* (design bureau)
KPA	(North) Korean People's Army
MBT	main battle tank
MORF	*Minoborony Rossiyskoy Federatsii* (Russian Ministry of Defence)
MOU	*Minoborony Ukrainy* (Ukrainian Ministry of Defence)
MRL	multiple rocket launcher
MRSI	multiple rounds simultaneous impact
NBC	nuclear, biological, and chemical
NHU	*Natsionalna hvardiia Ukrainy* (National Guard of Ukraine)
PGM	precision-guided munition
RAP	rocket-assisted projectile
RHA	rolled homogeneous armour
ROC	Republic of China, colloquially Taiwan
ROK	Republic of Korea, colloquially South Korea
SNS	satellite navigation system
SP	self-propelled
SPG	self-propelled gun
TrO	*Terytorialnoi oborony* (Territorial Defence Forces of Ukraine)
UAS	uncrewed/unmanned aerial system, colloquially 'drone'
USSR	Union of Soviet Socialist Republics
VSRF	*Vooruzhennie sily Rossiyskoy Federatsii* (Armed Forces of the Russian Federation)
VDV	*Vozdushno-desantnye voyska* (Soviet/Russian Airborne Forces)
ESU TZ	*Edinaya sistema upravleniya takticheskim zvenom* (Unified tactical level command & control system)
ZSU	*Zbroyini syly Ukrainy* (Armed Forces of Ukraine)

ACKNOWLEDGEMENTS

The author wishes to thank his NHU artilleryman acquaintance in Ukraine (who wishes to remain anonymous) for giving insight into how artillery is used on the battlefield and his experiences with *Giatsint*-B and other pieces. The author also wishes to thank Tom Cooper and David Bocquelet for their tremendous support in making this book a reality. The appearance of US Department of Defense (DOD) visual information does not imply or constitute DOD endorsement.

INTRODUCTORY NOTES

Cold War Soviet artillery pieces, including self-propelled guns and the guns they use, can have different designations and names. These can include the *Glavnoe raketno-artilleriyskoe upravlenie* (Main Rocket & Artillery Directorate, GRAU) index, a factory code, and/or a formal project name. Systems introduced before the 1960s are usually better known by their factory codes (e.g., the 152mm D-20 gun-howitzer, which also has the lesser-known GRAU index 53-P-546). More modern systems are usually known by their GRAU indices and/or project names instead (e.g. 2A36 *Giatsint*-B, 2S7 *Pion*). The author will generally prioritise using the project names, since these are less intimidating than indices or codes and are also typically the names used by troops, provided they exist. Second World War and earlier pieces were formally designated by their role and year of introduction (e.g. 76mm *divizionnaya pushka obr. 1942 g.* — '76mm divisional field gun model 1942'). This system was dropped in 1948, and today the factory code ('ZIS-3' in this case) is more commonly used.

The Soviet/Russian *Glavnoe bronetankovoe upravlenie* (Main AFV Directorate, GBTU) also assigns its own index to self-propelled artillery (e.g. the 2S7 *Pion* has the GBTU index '216' and is thus sometimes also called 'Object 216'). Strictly speaking, this index refers to the hull and automotive components: the gun and ammunition would fall under the GRAU system.

In addition to the barrel bore diameter (i.e. calibre), Western artillery guns are also often distinguished by the length of the barrel in calibres. Example: the M777 howitzer is often described as a

'155 mm L/39' howitzer, indicating that it has a bore diameter of 155mm and a barrel length of approximately 6.1m (39 calibres i.e. 155 x 39mm). The Soviets, Russians, and Ukrainians, on the other hand, did not and do not generally use this system. However, the author will adopt this shorthand generally to describe gun barrel length. Unless otherwise noted, this length does not include the muzzle brake.

Figures for shell velocities refer to the muzzle velocity. Due to air resistance and the laws of ballistics, shells will slow down in flight.

Soviet, Russian, and Ukrainian engines are rated in metric horsepower (1hp = 0.735kW). This is different to the imperial/mechanical horsepower commonly used in the US (1hp = 0.745kW). For consistency, metric horsepower will be used throughout the book.

For Soviet-designed artillery pieces, the emplacement/displacement time, i.e. time to bring a gun into/out of action, is provided as given in the manual. This time *does not* include the artillery survey time for laying the guns or preparing ammunition, which is included in Western emplacement time figures, thus they *cannot be directly compared.*

In the Soviet, Russian, and Ukrainian armies, what they call an 'artillery division' (*artdivizion*) is equivalent to an artillery battalion in Western militaries. This is *not* to be confused with 'divisional artillery', which are the integral artillery assets supporting a tank/motor-rifle division.

In the 'Context' sections, it will often be said that '[system] was intended for [purpose] in [unit type]'. It is very important to remember that, in practice, the distribution and use of these systems can vary *significantly* from the original intention, especially during wartime. Thus, these statements should be taken only as a general rule-of-thumb.

The numbers of Russian artillery pieces, unless otherwise noted, are taken from a 2012 table with a unit-by-unit breakdown given on Warfare.ru titled '*Osnovnyye vooruzheniya SV, VDV, BV VMF MO RF*' (archive.ph/rIi9T), which is the most comprehensive publicly available database for the *Vooruzhennie sily Rossiyskoy Federatsii* (Armed Forces of the Russian Federation, VSRF) artillery. The numbers are merely to provide context on the relative importance each type has had in the pre-war VSRF, and should *not* be taken as an accurate reflection of the situation today. The author(s) of the table themselves acknowledge that it is not 100 percent accurate and estimate that the real numbers could vary by no more than 20–25 percent. The real numbers may have also changed significantly over the following 10 years prior to the 2022 invasion as well as two years of high-intensity combat.

Loss numbers for both Russia (oryxspioenkop.com/2022/02/attack-on-europe-documenting-equipment.html) and Ukraine (oryxspioenkop.com/2022/02/attack-on-europe-documenting-ukrainian.html) are taken from the Oryxspioenkop website, which keeps a tally of visible losses. These numbers are likely to be underestimates, as artillery usually operates farther from the frontlines and there is less likely to be visual evidence of its loss.

As a final note, in the technical summaries, the radio equipment is listed as given in manuals or books, where available. However, during overhauls both pre- and post-1991, the radios could sometimes be switched out for newer ones. Soviet-legacy vehicles in Ukrainian service have mostly been upgraded with modern Western radios like Motorolas or less common L3Harris radios. Some Russian self-propelled guns (SPGs) may also have received new radios such as *Akveduk* (R-168) or *Abzats* (R-173) during refurbishment, although it is not unknown for Russian crews in Ukraine to also use Western walkie-talkie radios or GPS sets bought commercially.

INTRODUCTION

'Artilleriyskiy pot spasaet pekhotnuyu krov' ('Artillery sweat spares infantry blood')
— Vasyl Tadeyovych Kyrey (1926)

This epigraph appears in Kyrey's classic 1926 booklet *Artilleriya ataka i oborony* (*Artillery offence and defence*).[1] The phrase remains popular in both the Ukrainian and Russian militaries even today, and it reflects a fundamental 'truth': if the artillery cannot affect violence on the enemy, then it is up to the 'melee' weapons like the infantry and armour, with correspondingly increased casualties for them. As the planner of the 1916 Brusilov offensive's devastating artillery preparation, Kyrey well understood this fact; it is no accident that the Brusilov offensive is considered the Imperial Russian Army's most successful operation of the First World War.

Born in the city of Baturyn, today in Ukraine, Kyrey's background is rather illustrative of the complicated relationship between Ukraine and Russia. With the collapse of the Imperial Russian Empire in 1917 and the ensuing Russian Civil War, Kyrey would join the short-lived independent Ukrainian People's Republic before throwing his lot with Wrangel's White Russians. He was finally forced into exile in Czechoslovakia for the rest of his life following the Soviet Bolsheviks' final victory in the Russian Civil War and the creation of the Union of Soviet Socialist Republics (USSR), which also effectively destroyed any hope of an independent Ukrainian state.

Today's modern Ukraine and Russia were born in the aftermath of the USSR's own collapse in 1991. Unlike in 1917, this process was mostly peaceful. However, in the twenty-first century, as Russia seeks to reclaim its 'rightful' status as a great power, it has attempted to subjugate independent Ukraine under its dominion. Russia's annexation of Crimea in 2014 marked the beginning of the Russo-Ukrainian War, the largest conventional war in Europe since 1945. What started off as a hybrid war of plausible deniability in the Donbas would escalate into a full-scale invasion in 2022 that continues to this day, over 10 years after the Crimean annexation. However, what has not changed since 2014 is the dominant role that the artillery has played on the battlefield for both sides.

Throughout the Cold War, the USSR built up a formidable artillery arsenal that far exceeded NATO's quantitatively, if not qualitatively. This was partly a result of Soviet artillery doctrine, which stressed the importance of massed fires and pre-planned barrages as an enabler for breakthroughs and manoeuvre. Its collapse in 1991 saw this arsenal divided up among the successor states, with the Russian Federation inheriting the bulk of it. The Russian artillery arm significantly outnumbers its Ukrainian counterparts, and the relatively meagre successes enjoyed by the VSRF so far can often be at least partly attributed to its ability to simply throw more shells and explosives at the Ukrainians than the latter can throw back in return. To this end, it still heavily relies on its large inheritance of Soviet gun

Ukrainian gunner of the 55th 'Zaporizhzhian Sich' Artillery Brigade yells as a D-20 howitzer is fired, September 2014. One of the oldest Ukrainian artillery units, 55 Art. is considered an elite unit that has fought extensively since 2014. (55 Art.)

artillery systems and ammunition. As these have been progressively exhausted by attrition, Russia has even turned to the Democratic People's Republic of Korea (DPRK) to try to maintain this edge.

Ukraine has also inherited a considerable artillery arm from the USSR. However, much of it degraded along with other military infrastructure (such as ammunition production) over the years between independence and 2014, especially since Ukraine's military infrastructure was not subsidised by the West's energy imports the way Russia's was. Eight years of war in the Donbas also resulted in many systems becoming worn out without replacement. While Soviet-legacy gun artillery systems played a key role in blunting the initial 2022 invasion, they have since been supplemented or outright replaced by Western towed and self-propelled guns in some Ukrainian units. Nevertheless, Soviet systems continue to see service with other units of the *Zbroyini syly Ukrainy* (Armed Forces of Ukraine, ZSU) and National Guard of Ukraine (*Natsionalna hvardiia Ukrainy*, NHU), including pieces captured from the Russian military following their various defeats in 2022.

Despite the critical role gun artillery has played and continues to play in the Russo-Ukrainian War, the technical aspects and histories of the individual artillery systems used by both sides have received relatively little attention in English. They are often lumped together as generic 'artillery', which is understandable: unlike fighter planes or, to a lesser extent, tanks and other armoured vehicles, to most laypeople, an artillery gun is not very different from another one. The goal of this book is to attempt to shed more light on what makes each system special in its own way and how it contributes to this artillery-dominated war that continues to rage on at the time of writing.

This book is intended to be the first part of a two-book 'guide' to major gun artillery pieces in use during the Russo-Ukrainian War and focuses on Soviet-legacy designs used by both sides of the war. The artillery pieces described in this book fall into roughly three categories: guns, howitzers, and mortars. Latukhin's *Bog Voyny* offers some general characteristics for these, at least in Soviet terminology:[2]

- Gun: fires high-velocity shells with a relatively flat trajectory, usually with a long barrel. Usually optimised for direct fire or long-range counterbattery roles.
- Howitzer: fires heavier shells at lower velocities over an arcing trajectory at high elevation angles (in British parlance: 'upper register fire'). Relatively short barrel and light relative to the shell weight compared to a gun.
- Mortar: optimised for very high-elevation arcing trajectories, capable of dropping low-velocity projectiles (mortar bombs) near vertically on a target. Usually light for the projectile weight compared to guns or howitzers, but with much less range. Normally uses only a baseplate to absorb recoil, as opposed to a hydropneumatic/spring recoil absorption system found on almost all modern artillery pieces.

Table 1, reproduced from Latukhin, summarises these characteristics, though they are by no means strict rules:

Table 1: Artillery Characteristics

Type	Muzzle velocity (m/s)	Barrel length (calibres)	Gun/shell weight ratio
Gun	650–1,500	50–120	180–350
Howitzer	400–600	20–35	100–180
Mortar	100–350	10–25	15–30

Shell lethality is highly dependent on the impact angle due to the fragmentation pattern: at impact angles < 30° the fragmentation area is minimal, and almost negligible at < 20°.[3] Lower muzzle velocities result in larger impact angles: this is why howitzers are preferred as general-purpose artillery pieces, even though high-velocity guns have longer ranges. However, with variable charges, modern guns and howitzers can often perform each others' roles, and today the distinction between these two types is not so clear-cut. Indeed, some pieces (e.g. the *Nona* family) can perform all three roles.

Regrettably, due to the extraordinary variety of systems currently in use, the author will only be able to cover some of the more important ones in detail. This book will also not cover infantry mortars, as these are generally operated by infantrymen and are not usually found within artillery units, nor will it cover rocket artillery or tactical ballistic missiles; they would need their own volumes to describe adequately.

ARTILLERY FIRE CONTROL: A VERY BASIC PRIMER

At the most basic level, artillery indirect fire is a mathematical problem: what bearing (azimuth) and elevation (range) does the gun need to be pointed at to hit an unseen target, given the ballistic properties of its ammunition? The Imperial Russian Army were pioneers in modern indirect fire: in 1882, Imperial Russian officer Karl Guk published *Zakrytaya strelba polevoy artillerii* (*Indirect fire from field artillery*), one of the first books to tackle the problem of aiming the gun in bearing against an unseen target using trigonometry and reference points.[4] Since then, the science of indirect fire has been refined to levels that would have been unimaginable to Guk. This section only gives a very simplified, general overview of the indirect fire control problem and some of the tools used to solve it: specific practices can differ significantly between armies and over time.[5]

In order to be able to hit anything, an artillery battery has to both know its own location and the target's. Traditionally, upon arriving at a new firing position, an artillery survey must be conducted in order to fix the battery's position and orient it in some chosen direction. To do this, they are usually provided with surveying tools such as a map and the Soviet PAB-2 artillery director theodolite (or 'aiming circle' in American parlance), which is still used by Russian and Ukrainian artillery units.[6] This process usually takes several minutes, and is still done for older SPGs and most towed guns. Modern SPGs and some towed guns such as the M777A2 have inertial navigation systems (INS) and/or satellite navigation systems (SNS) integrated with their fire control systems (FCS), thus allowing them to maintain a real-time accurate track of their positions without external reference points or surveys. It is also possible to improvise using civilian GPS receivers for this purpose.

Target coordinates were usually obtained by forward observers, but today these have been almost completely replaced by unmanned aerial systems (UASs), ranging from purpose-built systems like the Turkish Bayraktar TB2 used by Ukraine and the Russian *Orlan* series on one end, to commercial quad-rotor drones such as the Chinese DJI Mavic series on the other. The latter can be operated by forward observer ground teams operating on the frontlines or even by the artillery units themselves. This targeting

Gunners of the Ukrainian 26th 'Roman Dashkevich' Artillery Brigade seen in October 2019 using Soviet-legacy tools for artillery surveys: the PAB-2 artillery director theodolite (left) and the DAK-2 laser rangefinder (right). Both are capable of measuring angles, the crucial ingredient needed for indirect fire targeting. The former is widely used by both sides. The latter is rarely used today: when the author showed this to his NHU artilleryman contact, he stated he had never seen nor used the DAK-2 before. (26 Art.)

data is usually relayed back to a command post controlling the artillery batteries. UASs are also used for adjusting fire, observing the fall of shots and 'walking' them on target. Some also function as laser designators for precision-guided munitions (PGMs) like *Krasnopol*. An excellent example of co-operation between UASs and artillery was the bombardment of Zmiinyi Island in the summer of 2022 by Ukrainian forces, which was conducted using French-supplied CAESARs and the Ukrainian *Bohdana* SPG prototype, with Bayraktars and Mavics as the spotters.[7]

Once these are known, the firing data can be calculated to give the bearing and elevation to be laid, as well as fuse settings. This must be corrected for internal (factors that affect muzzle velocity, e.g. barrel wear, projectile weight variations, charge temperature) and external (meteorological conditions, e.g. wind, pressure) ballistics. SPGs or towed guns without an onboard ballistic calculator or navigation system are reliant on external support like the 1V13 battery senior officer vehicle (equivalent to a British battery mobile command post or American fire direction centre (FDC)) to perform such calculations and broadcast the range and bearing settings. If these are not available, the gun crew would have to fall back on pre-calculated range tables. The data would then be used to lay the gun using its own sights: most Soviet-legacy artillery pieces use the D-726-45 mechanical sight with PG-1M panoramic periscope (in British parlance, these would be called a 'dial sight carrier' and 'dial sight', respectively). The former sets the elevation of the gun relative to the horizontal plane with the aid of an integral bubble level clinometer, while the latter sets the bearing. Modern SPGs and towed guns with INS/SNS, computerised fire controls, and ballistic calculators are capable of doing the entire fire control process autonomously, which significantly increases their accuracy and reaction speed and also allows them to operate in a very dispersed manner. They can generally be ready to fire within a minute of coming to a stop.

From the 1970s onwards, the Soviets integrated their artillery into fire control automation complexes (KAUO – *kompleks avtomatizirovannogo upravleniya ognyom*), the prototype of which is *Mashina* (1V12); it consists of a series of artillery command and reconnaissance vehicles (ACRVs) based on the MT-LBu tracked transporter which acquire targets and process them into firing data for SPG batteries under their control.[8] A similar complex, *Mashina*-B (1V17), was developed for towed and multiple rocket launcher (MRL) batteries, while the *Vozdushno-desantnye voyska* (Soviet/Russian Airborne Forces, VDV) received the *Reostat* (1V119), which performed the same functions. In response to the American TACFIRE system, greater automation was introduced with the *Faltset* (1V12M), which could transmit firing data directly to the *Msta*-S and modernised *Akatsiyas*. The Russians would continue to pursue greater automation of their self-propelled (SP) artillery, culminating in what are known as ASUNOs (*avtomatizirovannoy sistemy upravleniya navedeniyem i ognem* – 'automated targeting and fire control system') such as *Uspekh* (1V168), which finally gave their most advanced *Msta*-SM1/2 and *Akatsiyas* autonomous fire control capabilities mostly comparable with modern Western SPGs.[9] Together with modernised KAUOs such as *Mashina*-M and *Kapustnik* with improved processing capabilities, and networked by modern reconnaissance/command and control (C2) complexes like *Strelets* (83T251I) with supporting drones like *Orlan*-10, they form a potentially formidable and flexible reconnaissance-fires complex that is only limited by the reported lack of trained personnel to really take advantage of it, at least for now.[10]

Ukraine has taken a somewhat different approach, developing several C2 applications to network their artillery, the best known of which is the *Kropyva* software system. *Kropyva* consists of networked workstations and tablets running the eponymous software serving many functions.[11] In addition to navigation and mapping, it also contains an extensive database of artillery ammunition, obtains live meteorological data via a connection (if available) and uses this to calculate firing data for the chosen target and ammunition.[12] This means that, unlike the Russian ASUNOs, which are restricted to modernised SPGs, the Ukrainians can effectively give any towed or SP gun a ballistic calculator by providing it with a *Kropyva* tablet. It is also based on off-the-shelf technology, thus making it affordable for the Ukrainians to provide en masse to their forces and a very efficient force multiplier for even old towed guns like the D-20. It can even perform networking functions, though (contrary to popular media) according to the author's NHU acquaintance, it is not used as an 'Uber for artillery' network for fire direction (which is heavily centralised), but more as a battlefield awareness network for situational awareness. He states that in practice it is easier to just radio or signal in the fire coordinates than do it via *Kropyva*. This was further backed up by @prekrasnii1 of the 47th Mechanised Brigade, who stated to the author that he had never heard of anyone in this brigade use *Kropyva* for sending targeting information.

1

GODS OF WAR: SOVIET LEGACY ARTILLERY GUNS

The most evocative image of the *Bog Voyny* (God of War) originates in the Soviet era, from the Second World War to the Cold War: masses of guns and rockets that obliterate enemy defences, paving the way for rapid breakthroughs by the advancing mechanised units. As Chris Bellamy notes in his classic book *Red God of War*, while only comprising 15–25 percent of the Cold War-era Soviet Army's manpower, the artillery would provide 80 percent of the army's firepower.[1] The general perception of Soviet artillery as a highly destructive but inflexible tool remains commonly held, and it is still often applied to the modern Russian military. However, the reality both then and now is a lot more complicated, though this is a subject the author believes should be left to a more qualified author and a book of its own.[2]

Nevertheless, the postwar Soviet artillery arm would incorporate many lessons learned during the war. On the technical side, the Soviets were fortunate enough to have the gifted artillery designer Fyodor Petrov in their service. Petrov can justifiably be considered the 'John Browning' of Soviet artillery gun design: he led the development of nearly all major Soviet gun artillery pieces from 1936 to 1974, ranging from tank guns to howitzers. The weapons he designed, which include the D-20 and D-30 howitzers as well as the 125mm D-81 tank gun family, still perform stalwart

During the Second World War, the Soviets relied heavily on towed artillery for both direct and indirect fire support. They were also often used as anti-tank guns, as illustrated by the Panther burning in the background of the 76mm ZIS-3 divisional field gun (left). While the ZIS-3 was light enough to be pushed short distances by its crew, the heavy ML-20 required slow tractors like the S-65 *Stalinets*: many were lost in 1941 when the Germans overran them (right). (Mark Redkin; open sources, unknown photographer)

The popular image of Soviet artillery, as seen in the 1950 film *Padenie Berlina* (*The Fall of Berlin*): gun after gun lined up, preparing to hurl a barrage at the wave of a signal flag. The 152mm ML-20 seen here was the most important Soviet 152mm piece of the Second World War. (Mosfilm)

service on both sides of the Russo-Ukrainian War, 50 years after Petrov retired.

Nikita Khrushchev's rise to power in the 1950s would, however, result in a period of stagnation for Soviet artillery. Khrushchev sought to reduce the size of the USSR's conventional forces, relying on nuclear weapons and other new technologies instead. In particular, Khrushchev became convinced that missiles were the way of the future: in 1955, he exclaimed '*Artilleriya — eto peshchernaya tekhnika. Daeyush raketu!*' ('Artillery – this is cavemen's technology. Give me missiles!').[3] As a result, many promising projects for towed and SP guns were put on hold or cancelled.

Only Khrushchev's 'voluntary' retirement in 1964 and Leonid Brezhnev's rise to power, which brought a renewed emphasis on building up conventional forces to match the US, would see a reversal of this policy. By this time, Soviet military thinking had concluded that a strategic nuclear war between NATO and the Warsaw Pact was unlikely under the mutually assured destruction doctrine. However, tactical nuclear weapons use remained a real possibility during smaller scale wars, and SPGs, particularly ones capable of firing nuclear warheads, would be much better suited to such conflicts. Soviet SPGs in service up to this time were still Second World War leftovers such as the ISU-152 and SU-100. In 1965, a large-scale exercise was held at the Lvov (today Lviv, Ukraine) training grounds to assess their capabilities and found them completely unsuited to the modern battlefield.[4] Both had been primarily designed as direct-fire assault guns with limited gun elevation (~20°), more akin to the German *Sturmgeschütze*. This restricted their range and made them relatively poor indirect fire systems. They also could not maintain a high rate-of-fire due to the crew compartment filling up with asphyxiating gun fumes.

Simultaneously, the American M109 155mm SPG was already in service and would become the go-to SPG for most NATO (other than, predictably, France) and Western-aligned nations. The M109 was also supplemented by the long-range M107 175mm and heavy M110 203mm SPGs, and all three would prove their worth during the Vietnam War. As Uraltransmash general designer Yuri Tomashov noted:

> Only ten years later [after Khrushchev's 'cavemen technology' speech], during the Vietnam War, did the highest levels realize how far behind the US we were in the development of artillery. Then, the Americans first used the M109 SPGs, capable of hitting a target at a distance of 14 km. The USSR had nothing to answer.[5]

This urgent need to catch up would ultimately result in the classic Cold War Soviet 'flower' SPGs, so-called due to their project names, which entered service in the 1970s. The first of these were the 122mm *Gvozdika*, 152mm *Akatsiya*, and 240mm *Tyulpan*, soon followed by the 152mm *Giatsint* family and 203mm *Pion*.

The 1980s saw some efforts made towards consolidating the Soviet artillery arm around the 152mm *Msta* howitzer and 120mm *Nona* rifled mortar families. However, the Soviet collapse in 1991 left this process incomplete, and the large Soviet arsenal would end up divided among the successor states. 1992 Conventional Forces in Europe (CFE) treaty declarations indicate that Ukraine had 4,040 artillery pieces, while Russia had 6,415 in Europe, i.e. west of the Urals.[6] It has never been publicly established exactly how many artillery pieces the USSR had in 1991, but it has been estimated to be as high as 42,000 towed and SP pieces, the majority of which would have been in deep storage on Russian territory.[7]

The Soviets preferred a high degree of commonality between their towed and SP artillery guns to helped ease maintenance, production, logistics, and training: one of the lessons they took to heart from the Second World War. During the Cold War, these were sometimes developed simultaneously as part of what is known as a '*dupleks*'. An example of this is the *Msta dupleks*, which has towed (*Msta*-B, where 'B' denotes '*buksiruyemiy*' — 'towed') and SP (*Msta*-S, where 'S' denotes '*samokhodniy*' — 'self-propelled') parts.[8] Thus, the sections in this chapter combine the towed gun and its SP counterpart together due to their shared characteristics and development history.

As with tanks and aircraft, artillery pieces were normally designed by a specialised 'design bureau' (*konstruktorskoye byuro*, KB) which was hosted by a factory (*zavod*). There were several such organisations in the USSR during the Cold War, all of which still exist:

- Motovilikha (*Zavod* 172) and OKB-172, Perm
- Barrikady (*Zavod* 221) and OKB-221, Stalingrad (now Volgograd, Russia)
- *Zavod* 9 and OKB-9, Sverdlovsk (now Yekaterinburg, Russia)
- There were similar organisations that conducted SPG chassis development and production as well:

Soviet ISU-152M disabled during the 1956 Hungarian Revolution in Budapest (left); Fidel Castro's SU-100 during the Bay of Pigs invasion, Cuba, April 1961 (right). Dating back to the end of the Second World War, these were still the main SPGs used by Soviet Army up to the 1970s. (FOTO:FORTEPAN/ Nagy Gyula; Granma)

- Ural Transport Engineering Factory (*Uralskiy zavod transportnogo mashinostroeniya*, Uraltransmash) and OKB-3, Sverdlovsk
- Kirov Factory (*Leningrad Kirovskiy zavod*, LKZ) and KB-3, Leningrad (now St. Petersburg, Russia)
- Kharkov Tractor Factory (*Kharkovskiy traktorniy zavod*, KhTZ), Kharkov (now Kharkiv, Ukraine)

Some have changed names and been reorganised multiple times over the years (see the central section for a 'family tree'): for consistency, the names given above will be used to refer to these organisations in the Soviet historical context.[9]

2
D-20 & *AKATSIYA*: 152MM WORKHORSES

152mm D-20
Development History

Throughout the Second World War, the Red Army's primary 152mm artillery piece was the 152mm ML-20 howitzer-gun. It was designed by Petrov at OKB-172 in Molotov (later renamed Perm) in 1937 as part of a *dupleks* to serve alongside his 122mm A-19 corps gun in corps artillery regiments, with which it shared the same carriage.[1] The 7.2t ML-20 combined the characteristics of howitzers and guns through the use of variable charges and a high maximum gun elevation (up to +65°): its L/28 barrel could throw the standard 43.6kg OF-540 high explosive, fragmentation (HE-Frag) shell at 655m/s out to 17.2km, allowing it to outrange most 'pure' howitzers while still having the ability to attain high-elevation arcing trajectories using smaller charges. In addition to its use as a towed gun, the ML-20 would also be used to arm the SU-152 and ISU-152 SPGs.[2]

The Soviets also fielded smaller numbers of lighter 152mm howitzers like the new 152mm M-10 and modernised First World War 152mm howitzers within rifle and tank divisions as well as in

D-20 and its Ukrainian Marines crew, 2017. The D-20 was the most numerous towed 152mm artillery piece inherited by Ukraine from the USSR. (Telekanal 2+2)

152mm D-1 howitzer in action with Russian forces on the Vuhledar front, ca. February 2023, nearly 80 years after it first entered service. (MORF)

corps artillery. In theory, these howitzers would provide the divisions with an organic artillery asset more powerful than their 122mm howitzers. The German invasion inflicted particularly catastrophic losses on these howitzers: ~75 percent of those in service on 22 June 1941 were lost in 1941–1942.[3] Production of the M-10 had run into difficulties and was stopped in favour of the ML-20 by July 1941; the few survivors were relegated to the *Artilleriya rezerva Verkhovnogo Glavnokomandovaniya* (Supreme High Command artillery reserve, ARVGK) when the corps structure was abolished and 152mm howitzers were removed from divisional artillery in 1941. When the Red Army reestablished the corps structure in 1942, only a few hundred 152mm howitzers were left, and a replacement was much needed to arm these units.[4]

Meanwhile, Petrov had been transferred to Sverdlovsk in 1940 to setup mass production of his 122mm M-30 howitzer, where he would spend the rest of his career. After the German invasion, this artillery factory was amalgamated together with Leningrad's LKZ and Stalingrad's *Barrikady* factories following their evacuations to create *Zavod* 9 in 1942. Petrov would set up his own design bureau, OKB-9, at *Zavod* 9 that year; one of the first things he did was to start designing a new corps-level 152mm howitzer on his own initiative. Given the factory code 'D-1' ('D' for '*devyat*' — 'nine'), it was accepted into service in 1943.[5] At 3.6t, the more mobile D-1 could be towed by Lend-Lease Studebaker trucks.[6] Its L/25 barrel could throw the 40kg OF-530 HE-Frag shell at 655m/s out to 12.4km.[7] Although the D-1 is commonly seen as a Second World War howitzer, in fact relatively few were built during the war, with most production occurring in the immediate postwar years.[8]

In the immediate aftermath of the war, Petrov began work on replacements for the D-1, A-19, and ML-20. In a development process historian Aleksandr Shirokorad describes as 'extremely confusing', Petrov started off with a '*tripleks*' of guns in the 5t range, comprising a 100mm anti-tank (AT) gun (D-70), 122mm corps gun (D-71), and 152mm corps howitzer (D-72), all sharing the same carriage. Only the latter two would eventually reach production as the 122mm D-74 and 152mm D-20 in 1953.[9] The D-20/D-74 had a high degree of commonality, to the extent that they were originally issued with the same service manual covering both. The most significant difference was the barrels: 122mm L/47 (D-74) and 152mm L/25 (D-20). The former comes with an adapter sleeve, allowing both barrels to be mated to the same breech.[10]

Simultaneously, another *dupleks* was being offered by Mikhail Tsiryulnikov's team at Petrov's old workplace in Perm: the famous 130mm M-46 (see *Giatsint* section) and its lesser-known partner, the 152mm M-47. Both were significantly more powerful weapons with longer ranges, but this came at the cost of weight: approximately 50 percent more than Petrov's guns. The Soviets would end up adopting all four pieces: the D-20 as a corps-level weapon and the M-47 built in small numbers for the ARVGK and army-level artillery regiments, thus both ended up covering the ML-20's roles separately.[11]

The D-20 went on to become a standard divisional and corps-level 152mm weapon of the Soviet Army for most of the Cold War, and even today can still be found in use with both Ukrainian and Russian forces.[12] It was also widely exported to the Warsaw Pact and other Soviet-friendly states. The D-74 would also be exported and was even built in the People's Republic of China (PRC) as the Type 60 field gun, though its career in the Soviet Army was relatively brief, having been mostly superseded by the M-46. In 1981, the Soviet service manual was issued for only the D-20, suggesting that

122mm D-74 captured by US Marines in Vietnam during Operation Dewey Canyon being prepared for shipment to the USMC Museum, 1969 (left). Ukrainian 152mm D-20 prepares to be towed by a KrAZ truck, October 2020 (right). The D-74 has a significantly longer barrel than the D-20, but is otherwise nearly identical visually. (USMC Archives; ZSU)

the D-74 was out of Soviet service by then. However, in October 2024 the D-74 made a surprise re-appearance when the *Minoborony Rossiyskoy Federatsii* (Russian Ministry of Defence, MORF) released a video of the gun in service with Russian forces in Ukraine.[13] It is not known if the gun was retrieved from deep Russian storage left from the Cold War or came from the DPRK, PRC, or Iran, all of which are known users of the gun.

Technical Summary

The D-20 is officially described as a 'gun-howitzer' in the manual and firing tables. The carriage restricts its elevation to +45°, limiting its use as a howitzer and thus apparently giving it more similar properties to a field gun in the eyes of the GRAU.[14] It weighs 5.65t in combat position, and is light enough to be towed by a Ural-375D 6x6 truck. The L/25 monobloc barrel is capped with a massive muzzle brake to help dissipate the powerful recoil. This results in a considerable amount of overpressure for the crew as some of the muzzle blast is redirected to the sides of the gun, but the trade-off was accepted by the Soviets in order to allow the gun to be mated to a lighter carriage and recoil mechanism. It is ballistically identical to the ML-20 and designed to use the same range of 152mm ammunition. A semi-automatic vertical-sliding-block breech is used instead of the interrupted screw breech of the ML-20 and D-1, allowing for a faster rate-of-fire (5–6 rounds/minute vs. 3–4 of older 152mm guns).

A mechanical sight (S71-type) with panoramic periscope (PG-1) for indirect fire and a telescopic sight (OP-4) for direct fire are provided. On most previous Soviet artillery guns, the elevation and traverse controls were on opposite sides of the gun, designed for two-man gun-laying. This meant that aiming the gun required careful coordination between two gunners, a significant challenge when engaging moving targets like tanks, resulting in poor accuracy if the crew were not well-trained. The D-20 and all future Soviet artillery pieces would have the sights, elevation and traverse controls on the left side, allowing aiming to be done by only one person.

The carriage is of a relatively conventional split-trail type with spades. Particularly noteworthy are the pedestal with a hydraulic jack at the front of the carriage and roller wheels on each trail. When deployed, the gun rests on the pedestal and trails with

D-20 of the Ukrainian 59th 'Yakiv Gandzyuk' Motorised Brigade being fired by a gunner using a lanyard from a dug-out, a common practice to minimise exposure to the muzzle blast, March 2017. (MOU)

Ukrainian Marine gunner aims his D-20 with the PG-1 panoramic periscope of its S71-97 mechanical sight, August 2017. The round holder is for the OP-4 telescopic sight: it is not fitted as it is not useful for indirect fire. (Dmytro Udovytskyi, MOU)

the wheels raised above ground and angled outwards to take the load off their torsion bar suspensions and provide a more steady platform; however, this is not always done out of expediency. The pedestal and trail rollers enable the crew to rapidly shift fire beyond the actual traverse of the mount (+/-29°). This feature was apparently inspired by American 155mm Howitzer M1 (later M114); though it had not been sent under Lend-Lease, Soviet designers were aware of its existence and features.[15] The carriage and solid foam rubber tires allow towing on roads at up to 60km/h. The D-20 is normally serviced by a crew of seven and it is expected to take no more than 2–2.5 minutes to emplace/displace the 5.7t gun.

Akatsiya

Development History

Uraltransmash was tasked with making a new SPG to replace the wartime SU-76M in Soviet tank division artillery regiments as early as 1947. Although sometimes used during the war in the indirect fire support role, the SU-76M was no better suited for it than the aforementioned SU-100 and ISU-152 with its 15° gun elevation. Furthermore, its 76mm ZIS-3 field gun was considered too light in firepower. Development was initially helmed by Lev Gorlitskiy at OKB-3 until he moved back to Leningrad in 1953 and was replaced by Georgiy Yefimov. Designated SU-100P (GBTU: 105), it was armed with the 100mm D-50/D-10A, based on Petrov's D-10 gun

Left: manual jack used to raise or lower trails. Right: trail roller wheels used to assist the crew when moving the trails or rotating the entire gun to shift fire. Like most Soviet towed artillery, the D-20 does not have an APU or hydraulics to assist with movement. (ZSU)

Ukrainian *Akatsiya* during a coastal defence exercise on the Azov Sea coast, December 2019. These were the most common Ukrainian SPGs in 2014 and remained the backbone of Ukrainian tank/mechanised brigade artillery units until Western systems began arriving after the 2022 invasion. (ZSU)

that armed the SU-100 and T-54. Unlike older SPGs, the lightly armoured SU-100P's chassis was completely new and not based on an existing tank. It had its gun mounted on an open shielded mount with wide traverse and elevation (up to +37°) arcs. This gave it an indirect fire range of 14.8km, and allowed a rapid rate-of-fire to be maintained without choking the crew on gun gases.[16]

The new platform was also tested with other weapons, including the SU-152G (GBTU: 108) variant with a modified version of the D-1 howitzer.[17] Both the SU-100P and SU-152G were accepted into service in 1955, just in time to be killed off by Khrushchev as 'cavemen's technology' that same year.[18] Fortunately for Uraltransmash, the Object 105 chassis would find other uses such as a carrier for the *Krug* ('Circle') surface to air missile system (2K11): these were the 2P24 (GBTU: 123) TEL and 1S32 (GBTU: 124) missile guidance radar vehicles. Thus, when the Soviets came back around to developing a new generation of SPGs, the Object 123/124 chassis was already in production and suitable for adaptation.[19] It was chosen for the *Akatsiya* ('Acacia') project, which was authorised for full-scale development in 1967. OKB-3 and OKB-9 were tasked with developing the vehicle (GRAU: 2S3; GBTU: 303) and gun (D-22; GRAU: 2A33), respectively.[20] The first prototypes were completed in 1968, but problems with propellant gas contamination and other systems delayed service entry until 1971.[21, 22]

SU-100P (left) and SU-152G (right) at the Kubinka Tank Museum, Russia. Other prototypes based on the versatile SU-100P chassis can be seen in the background. (Alan Wilson)

2P24 TEL of the *Krug* surface to air missile system at the Ukrainian Air Force Museum, Vinnitsa (left). Early prototype *Akatsiyas* (right) used the front half of the hull virtually unchanged, with one fewer road wheel in the suspension. (George Chernilevsky; War-book.ru)

After ~200 vehicles produced, the *Akatsiya* was modernised to the 2S3M standard, which entered service in 1975 and became the most common variant.[23] The 2S3M1 (GBTU: 303M1) with automated targeting data reception was introduced into service in 1987. This equipment put it on a similar level of fire control as the basic *Msta*-S, which was also entering service at the time, but 2S3M1s were only built in relatively small numbers due to production problems with the data receiver.[24] Production continued at Uraltransmash until 1993.[25] The latest Russian 2S3M2 (GBTU: 303M2) upgrade from 2004 introduced the *Uspekh* (1V168-1) automatic FCS and datalink with GLONASS integration, bringing existing 2S3M/M1s up to par with the *Msta*-SM1/2 in terms of fire control and allowing them to be integrated into the ESU TZ (*Edinaya sistema upravleniya takticheskim zvenom*, Unified tactical level command & control system) battlefield management system (BMS).[26] This does not appear to be a common upgrade, with the first batch only being announced delivered in 2021.[27] Because of the relatively few original 2S3s and 2S3M2s produced, it can be assumed that the *Akatsiyas* in service with both Ukraine and Russia today are of the 2S3M/M1 standard. Thus, the following technical summary will only describe these in detail. It is not possible to tell 2S3M/M1 apart without looking inside the SPG, for there are no external differences.

Technical Summary

The *Akatsiya* is armed with the 152mm 2A33 (D-22) howitzer, adapted from the D-20 with only minor changes, most notably a fume extractor to reduce gun gases entering the turret. It is ballistically identical to the D-20, but the *Akatsiya* can also elevate its gun higher up to 60°, allowing it to shoot in higher arcing trajectories. The turret

Russian *Akatsiya* upgraded to 2S3M2 standard seen during rehearsals for the 2009 Victory Day parade in Yekaterinburg, Russia, where Uraltransmash and *Zavod* 9 are based. It is most easily recognised by the SNS antenna between the commander's cupola and radio antenna. This is the most modern variant of the *Akatsiya* in Russian service, though it is not commonly seen. (Falshivomonetchik)

Ukrainian *Akatsiya* conducts direct fire during an artillery competition, August 2019 (left). *Akatsiya* being used for training Russian mobilised personnel in the Khmelevka Baltic Fleet training ground, Kaliningrad, 2023 (right). Direct fire using artillery is rarely done in actual combat, but many armies still train for it just in case. (ArmyTV; MORF)

employs a 2E24 electromechanical elevation/traverse drive and has 360° traverse for rapid reaction all-round fire. Indirect fire aiming is done with the PG-4 panoramic periscopic sight, while direct fire is conducted using the OP5-38 telescopic sight. The communications suite of the 2S3M (as of 1980) consisted of the *Magnolia*-M (R-123M) radio and *Lebed* (1V116) crew intercom.

The 2S3M1 upgrade integrated the *Akatsiya* with the *Mekhanizator* (1V514) complex. *Mekhanizator* consists of two equipment pieces: the 1V518 automated transceiver found on 1V13M platoon command vehicles (part of the *Faltset* (1V12M), i.e. modernised *Mashina* (1V12), artillery fire control complex), and the 1V519 receiver, which is mounted in the upgraded *Akatsiyas*.[28]

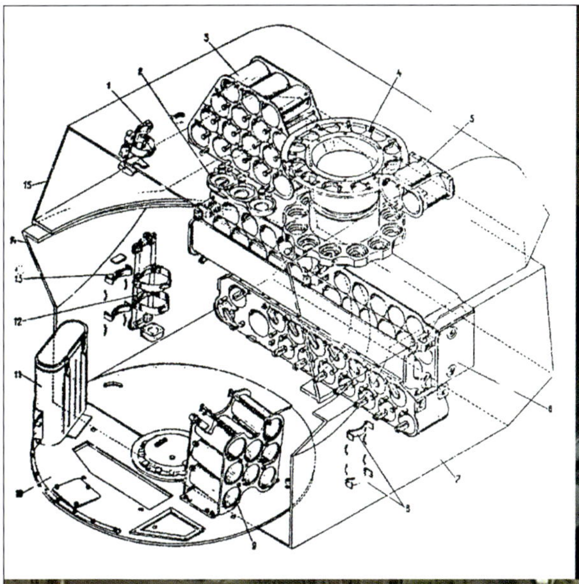

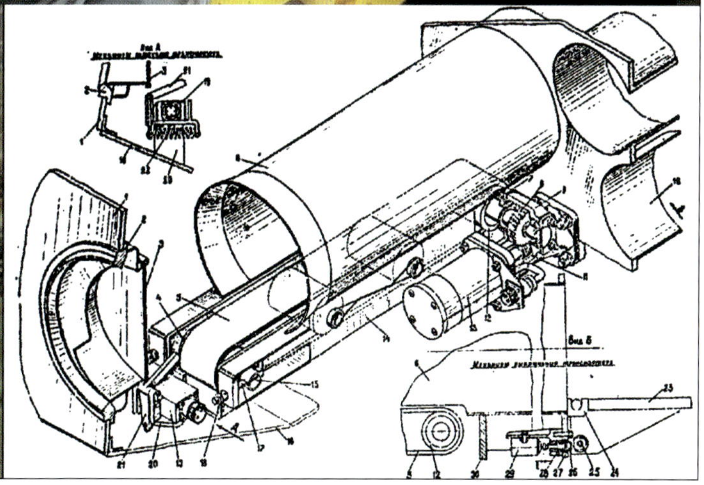

Top left: ammunition stowage on the *Akatsiya* (2S3M) from the manual. The original 2S3 had automatic loading for the shells, but this was eliminated in subsequent variants. Top right: the 12-round mechanised carousel in the turret assists the loader with retrieving heavy shells, though both the shells and charges must be placed manually in the gun rammer. The other racks in the turret rear are for charges. Bottom: Ukrainian cadets demonstrate passing rounds into an *Akatsiya* through the loading hatch (A). The rounds are sent into the lower hull via a mechanised 'transporter' (B), where the loader will pick them up. (Author's collection; Igor Zakharenko; (A) Militarnyi; (B) author's collection)

Top: the *Akatsiya* has a rammer to assist the loader, who must manually place the projectile into it before activating the rammer, and then repeats for the charge. Once finished, the rammer will withdraw, leaving space for the gun to recoil into and eject the spent charge case. Bottom: the turret side hatch has a small circular hatch through which the loader can push out spent cases for better sealing in NBC conditions, although it is more common in practice to just open the entire hatch to do this. The remote-controlled PKT can be seen on top. (VoenTV Belarus; MORF)

It allows the *Faltset* complex to transmit targeting data directly to the 2S3M1, allowing them to fire PGMs such as *Krasnopol* in an automated mode. It also significantly improves the reaction times of the battery when compared to the original *Mashina* complex. For example, the time to engage an unplanned target was reduced from six to four minutes, and the deployment time from 12 to 10 minutes. In addition, the 2S3M1 also received the 1P5 panoramic sight, in which the gunner would enter the sight settings received via *Mekhanizator* to aim the gun, thus reducing the likelihood of error.[29]

A maximum of 46 shells and charges each are carried onboard. The *Akatsiya* can naturally fire any projectiles developed for the D-20 or ML-20, but by the 1970s, new projectiles were being introduced as well: these included the 3OF25 *Grif* HE-Frag with increased explosive filler and 3OF22 *Kren* RAP, which extended the maximum range from 17.4km to 20.5km. The maximum rate-of-fire using the turret ammunition is 3.5 rounds/minute, dropping down to 2.6 for the hull ammunition, with the average rate-of-fire for all 46 rounds at 1.9 rounds/minute. A rammer attached to the breech rams shells and charges into the gun once the loader places them into the tray. On the right side of the turret is a large hatch through which the loader can dispose of spent charge cases. A 'transporter' conveyor is located in the rear hull for supplying ammunition from outside the vehicle. A rate-of-fire of 3.4 rounds/minute can be attained using this method. The *Akatsiya* can also fire BP-540 high explosive, anti-tank (HEAT) or BR-540/540B armour-piercing (AP) shells against tanks, although these rounds are uncommon today.

The commander's cupola has a remotely controlled 7.62mm PKT anti-aircraft machine gun (AAMG) mounting that can be aimed and fired from under armour, primarily intended for self-defence against low-flying aircraft or infantry. A total of 1,500 rounds are carried. The fully enclosed turret and hull protects the crew of four against small arms fire and shell fragments: 30mm thick on the turret and hull front, 15mm elsewhere.[30] The *Akatsiya* also has a retractable dozer blade in the front of the vehicle for digging defensive emplacements. Unusually, the emplacement/displacement time is not given in the manual.

The 27.5t *Akatsiya* is powered by a 520hp V-59U longitudinally placed in the front of the vehicle next to the driver providing a respectable power-weight ratio of 19hp/t. It is a derivative of the ubiquitous V-2 family of V-12 four-stroke diesel engines that has powered many Soviet armoured fighting vehicles (AFVs) dating back to the Second World War, such as the T-34. The front transmission

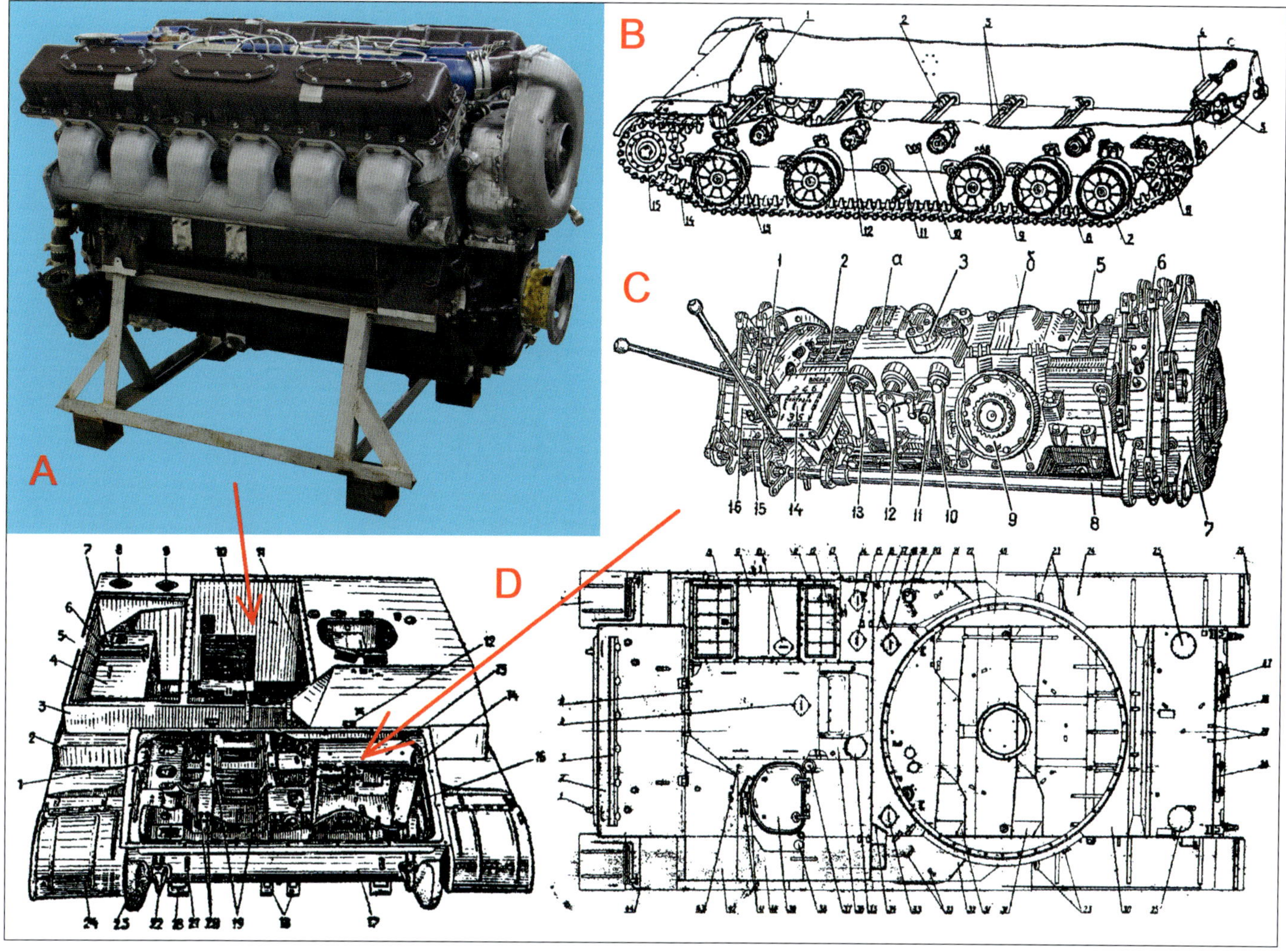

V-59U engine (A), suspension (B), transmission (C), and hull layout (D), with arrows showing where the engine and transmission go. The *Giatsint*-S and *Tyulpan* are identical to the *Akatsiya* automotively. ((A) Argun Kazakhstan; (B-D) author's collection)

is of a dual-flow hydromechanical type with planetary steering gears on the left and right sides. This gives it (as well as other vehicles based on the Object 123 chassis) a rare feature among Soviet AFVs: neutral steering, i.e. the ability to put one set of tracks in reverse and the other forward, allowing the *Akatsiya* to rotate in place. It has six forward + two reverse gears, giving a maximum road speed of 60km/h. The suspension is of a conventional torsion bar type, with six rubber-rimmed road wheels, four return rollers, and single-pin 'live' tracks with rubber bushings. There are two telescoping hydraulic shock absorbers on each side, on the first and last road wheel assemblies.

Context

As the workhorses of Soviet divisional artillery regiments throughout the Cold War, it is hardly surprising that both the D-20 and *Akatsiya* are being used in significant numbers by Ukraine and Russia. The D-20 is more reminiscent of a Second World War artillery piece: there are no 'extras' one might find on newer towed guns such as an auxiliary power unit (APU) for limited autonomous movement, load-assist devices, hydraulic power to assist with emplacing/displacing the gun, or digital displays/fire controls. Everything depends on the strength and skill of its crew. The *Akatsiya*, on the other hand, was a relatively advanced SPG for the 1970s and is very similar to the primary NATO SPG of the time, the M109. Alongside the *Gvozdika*, it represented a quantum leap in capability for Soviet tank/mechanised artillery units.

The *Msta*-B/S 152mm towed/SP guns were intended to replace the older D-20/*Akatsiyas* , but the USSR's collapse in 1991 prevented this. It is known that approximately 3,700 D-22 howitzers were built by the Motovilikha and Barrikady factories.[31] Some of these guns would have been reserved for spare parts, but conservatively estimating 25 percent kept as spares would still leave approximately at least 2,800 *Akatsiyas* produced, compared to an estimated 1,130 *Msta*-Ss produced up to 2019.[32] In 2012, it was estimated that there were 955 Akatsiyas in service across 29 Russian units. The *Akatsiya* still forms a significant part of the various Russian forces fighting today in Ukraine. This is also reflected in the losses sustained by the type, second only to the *Msta*-S family among SPGs at the time of writing. Prior to and during the early stages of the 2022 invasion, the D-20 was more commonly found in the Luhansk/Donetsk militias.[33] It was not seen in VSRF service prior to 2022 and most, if not all, were believed to have been in deep storage, with only 106 listed active in 2012. However, it has now been seen with 'proper' Russian forces as more are withdrawn from storage to make up for attrition.[34]

The D-20 and *Akatsiya* are, numerically, the most important 152mm pieces inherited by Ukraine from the USSR, at 215 and 501, respectively. The D-20 was retired from Ukrainian service in 2013, but hastily brought back after the war began in 2014, while the *Akatsiya* was the standard SPG for tank and mechanised brigades in 2014.[35] [36] Ukraine has lacked the funds or means to do much beyond refurbishment. Sustaining the *Akatsiya* is further complicated by the fact that the chassis production is based in Russia, thus sourcing parts and maintaining the *Akatsiya* is

Ukrainian *Akatsiyas* with white recognition markings being monitored by the Organization for Security and Co-operation in Europe's SMMU (Special Monitoring Mission to Ukraine) as they withdraw from the Donbas front, March 2015. Under the terms of the Minsk II ceasefire, both sides were required to withdraw artillery pieces with a calibre greater than 100mm at least 50km from the line of contact. (OSCE)

more difficult for the Ukrainians. It is reasonable to expect that, as the existing vehicles and barrels are worn out, they will be progressively replaced by NATO 155mm pieces that Ukraine has started receiving since the 2022 Russian invasion or the domestically produced *Bohdana*.

Both the D-20 and *Akatsiya* are obsolescent by today's standards. They are heavily outranged by modern NATO 155mm L/39 and L/52 pieces, which have more range using standard shells (24–30km) than the former can attain using rocket-assisted projectiles (RAPs). The short range also means they must be placed closer to the frontline, with increased risks from enemy counterbattery action or, more recently, UASs such as first person view (FPV) drones. There is also some anecdotal evidence that they are less accurate than newer guns like the NATO or later Soviet pieces: the author was told by a Ukrainian artilleryman in the NHU that his unit once received D-20s, but they were sent away due to their poor accuracy. While this can be counteracted with PGMs such as *Krasnopol*, they are expensive and relatively uncommon. While there have been deep upgrades proposed for the *Akatsiyas* still in Russian service, for the most part, Russia has focused its efforts on the *Msta*-S and its own planned successor, *Koalitsiya*-SV. The most recent 2S3M2 upgrade does not do anything to close the substantial range gap between the *Akatsiya* and modern NATO systems, and is fairly uncommon.

Russian *mobiks* of the Western Military District prepare to fire a D-20 at Ukrainian positions, April 2023. These older weapons were brought out of storage in order to both replace losses and fulfil the materiel needs of the expanded Russian military following the 'partial mobilisation'. The barrel bears the name '*Varvara*'. (MORF)

For all their obsolescence, the D-20 and *Akatsiya* are nevertheless tough, simple, and reliable weapons. The brute explosive power of a 152mm HE shell is not to be underestimated, and ultimately, a gun is merely a conduit for shells. It is rarely a bad thing to have more barrels to throw more shells at the enemy. New assets like the Ukrainian *Kropyva* defence mapping software and prolific UAS spotters such as the Russian *Orlan*-10 also allow these venerable pieces to be more effective than ever before in well-trained hands. As long as there are barrels, shells, and parts for them, they will probably find some use in a war where both sides can never have too much artillery.

3

D-30 & *GVOZDIKA*: 'FROG' BY NAME, 'FROG' BY NATURE

122mm D-30

Development History

Petrov's 122mm M-30 howitzer was the standard Soviet and Warsaw Pact divisional howitzer from the Second World War to the 1950s. It was a conventional split-trail design with a 122mm L/23 barrel, capable of firing the standard 21.8kg OF-462 shell at 515m/s out to 11.7km, and a combat weight of ~2.5t.[1] During the war, it was not uncommon for M-30s to fight against tanks, especially in the earlier years. Like the D-1, the M-30 had serious limitations in the role, including the two-man gun-laying controls and lack of an accurate direct fire sight: in one trial, an M-30 crew failed to hit a captured tank at 500m even once with 15 shells. The M-30's weight and limited traverse (49°) also made it difficult to shift fire quickly. The M-30 subsequently saw combat during the Korean War, where its limitations were once again put on display.[2]

Reserve officer cadets training to conduct indirect fire with a D-30A at the Ivan Cherniahovskyi National Defence University of Ukraine, August 2018 (MOU).

122mm M-30 howitzer battery of the 2nd Ukrainian Front prepares to open fire in Hungary, 1944. Designed in the 1930s, the M-30 remains in service with several countries, and at least one has been seen in Russian service in Ukraine. (TASS (public domain))

In 1954, Petrov's OKB-9 was tasked with the replacement. The new 122mm howitzer was to have longer range and be able to shift fire quickly in all directions. Initially, to meet the latter requirement, a layout similar to the D-20 using a pedestal was considered, but this was discarded in favour of a tripod carriage that promised a shorter reaction time.[3] Ballistically, the new howitzer would fall between the M-30 howitzer and A-19 corps gun, giving it a longer range than the M-30 while retaining the ability to fire in high-arcing trajectories. Development of the 122mm D-30 (GRAU: 2A18) took place around the time of Khrushchev's 'missile era'; fortunately for the D-30, due to a combination of its innate technical qualities and Petrov's deft handling of the potentially volatile political atmosphere, it was one of the few Soviet artillery projects to survive the Khrushchev premiership.[4]

The D-30 was accepted into service in 1960 after a prolonged testing period, marking the beginning of a long and extremely successful career by any measure.[5] Built in large numbers, the D-30 would be exported to the far corners of the world, and has been involved in almost every significant military conflict that has occurred since it first entered service. Relatively few modifications were made to the D-30 over its long career; the most significant of these was the D-30A (GRAU: 2A18M), introduced in 1978 with a new muzzle brake and miscellaneous small improvements.[6] In general, most D-30s seen in the Russo-Ukrainian War are D-30As, though as attrition burns through these guns the older D-30 is becoming more common.

Technical Summary

The D-30A uses a monobloc L/35 barrel: with a full charge, it is capable of throwing the standard 21.8kg 3OF24 *Voron* ('Crow') HE-Frag shell at 690m/s out to a maximum range of 15.3km. The D-30A can also fire some older projectiles made for the M-30, but it is not rated for the M-30's weaker charges. A semi-automatic vertical-sliding block breech is used with a specified 6–8 rounds/minute maximum rate-of-fire, higher than the M-30's 5–6 rounds/minute with an interrupted screw breech. The original D-30's slotted muzzle brake dissipates ~50 percent of the recoil energy, allowing for a lighter recoil mechanism and carriage.[7] On the D-30A, it is a double-baffle type similar to the D-20's, instead of the original D-30's slotted one. This reduced the muzzle brake's recoil dissipation but also reduced the overpressure created by firing the gun in the crew's surroundings, which for the original D-30 was twice as much as would be considered acceptable in a Western army.[8]

As a howitzer, the D-30A can elevate up to 70° to attain the requisite high-arcing trajectories. However, it can only do so when the gun breech is not directly over one of the legs. If it is, the elevation is restricted to 18° by a mechanical cam in order to prevent the recoiling breech striking the leg and potentially damaging the breech.[9] The primary indirect fire sighting device is the D-726-45 mechanical sight with PG-1M panoramic periscope (hereafter 'D-726-45/PG-1M'). Direct fire aiming is primarily done with the OP-4M-45 telescopic sight. The D-30 has a reputation for good accuracy among Soviet guns, even sometimes referred to as an 'artillery sniper rifle', but it is difficult to judge without hard data for comparable guns.[10]

The tripod carriage is easily the most unique feature of the D-30 family. It is also responsible for the nickname sometimes given to the D-30: *Lyagushka* ('Frog').[11] It consists of a small circular platform in the middle with one fixed leg and one movable leg on each side. In traveling configuration, the legs are folded and clamped together with the barrel pointing over them. The muzzle brake has a towing hook attached to it, a feature the D-30A shares with the American

NHU D-30 at the full recoil stroke, firing at Russian units in the Kharkiv sector, October 2022. This is an original D-30 from the 1960s with slotted muzzle brake and hinged tow linkage. Some of these guns were brought out of storage post-2014 and put back into service. (NHU East)

Russian *mobiks* from the 2022 'partial mobilisation' training to use a 122mm D-30A for direct fire at the Central Military District training ground in Novosibirsk, November 2022. Right: D-726-45/PG-1M sight. This sight can also be used for direct fire if the telescopic sight (grey tube) is non-functional. (MORF; NHU)

M777. Deployed, the wheels are raised and the two movable legs folded out to 120° and fixed with pins. A hydraulic jack is built into the platform to assist getting into/out of position. It takes 1.5–2.5 minutes for the crew of seven to emplace/displace a D-30.[12]

The entire howitzer weighs ~3.2t, light enough to be towed by a 4x4 truck or MT-LB multipurpose tractor/armoured personnel carrier (APC). However, the listed prime mover for the D-30A in the 1988 manual is the ZIL-131 6x6 truck. The D-30A has pneumatic rubber tires, which allow a higher towing speed (80km/h) than the original D-30's solid foam rubber tires (40km/h). The D-30A also has turning indicators and brake lights on its shield for convenience and road safety reasons when towing the gun in a column.[13]

Gvozdika

Development History

While Uraltransmash worked on the *Akatsiya*, development of the *Gvozdika* ('Carnation') 122mm SPG was assigned to KhTZ's internal KB under Anatoliy Belousov. The VNII-100 research institute had previously identified three chassis to base it on: the BMP-1 (GBTU: 765), MT-LB (GBTU: 6), and Object 123/124.[14]

(A) In traveling configuration, the D-30's tripod legs are folded together and the barrel clamped to the legs, minimising the overall length. (B) To emplace, the D-30 is set on a pedestal (round on the D-30, rectangular on the D-30A) and the wheels raised using levers. (C) The legs are then spread out and the howitzer lowered to the ground. (D) Stakes can then be hammered into the legs for added stability. (129th TrO Brigade; TRK Zvezda; MOU; ZSU)

Ukrainian *Gvozdika* of the 36th 'Mykhailo Bilinskyi' Marine Brigade, seen during Exercise Sea Breeze 2019 on the Black Sea coast. The *Gvozdika*'s light weight has made it the SPG of choice for Soviet, Russian, and Ukrainian marines. (ZSU)

The 123/124 chassis was considered too heavy and was also not amphibious, thus it was rejected. The BMP version was also not pursued for some reason: it may have had to do with the ChTZ (*Chelyabinskiy traktorniy zavod* – 'Chelyabisnk tractor factory'; the BMP's manufacturer) 'categorical refusal to use BMPs for the placement of special equipment'.[15] The choice thus defaulted to KhTZ's MT-LB tracked transporter.

It was then found that the MT-LB chassis could not handle the weight, and development switched to a stretched version with an extra roadwheel: the future MT-LBu (GBTU: 10). The chassis developed for the *Gvozdika* is known as the MT-LBush (GBTU: 26), and it is unified with the *Meteorit* (UR-77) mine-clearing line charge launcher. The 122mm D-32 (GRAU: 2A31) was adapted from the D-30 by OKB-9 for the *Gvozdika*, again under Petrov. The first prototypes were completed and tested in 1969. Like the *Akatsiya*, problems were encountered with gas build-up in the turret: during one test, the gas build-up in the turret after firing eight rounds nearly killed the gunner and loader, who had to be hospitalised. These were

The MT-LB is often used as a prime mover for the D-30 howitzer, as seen here. Unsung workhorses of the Soviet and today's Russian and Ukrainian armies, the MT-LB family's chief designer Anatoliy Belousov (top left) is mostly forgotten today. (ZSU; Kharkiv Chamber of Commerce & Industry)

solved with an improved gun fume extractor and charge cases with better obturation (sealing of the gun breech). The *Gvozdika* was accepted into service in 1970 with mass production beginning the following year.[16]

Like the D-30, *Gvozdikas* would be widely exported both within and outside the Warsaw Pact. In addition to Soviet production, the *Gvozdika* was also licence-built in Bulgaria and Poland. Bulgarian *Gvozdikas* are essentially identical to Soviet ones (although of reputedly poorer build quality, according to Knyazev).[17] In Poland, the *Gvozdika* is known as the *Goździk*. These have received upgrades such as integration with the highly advanced *Topaz* automated fire control and command system and the 2S1-M variant with improved floatation kits and propellers to improve their amphibious capabilities.[18] [19] Both countries have sent some of these pieces to Ukraine as aid since the 2022 invasion.

Some Russian *Gvozdikas* have also been modernised in an analogous way to the *Akatsiya*'s 2S3M2 upgrade to the 2S1M1 standard with the 1V168-1 automated FCS with GLONASS integration, though the author has rarely come across photos or videos of these so far.[20] There is also the *Khosta* ('Hosta', 2S34), which is essentially a Russian deep modernisation of the *Gvozdika* from 2003 with a 120mm 2A80 rifled mortar instead of the D-32 howitzer; these are also very rare, with only several dozen estimated to be in service (at least 50 by 2015).[21] [22] The technical summary will focus on the Soviet-legacy *Gvozdikas*, as they are the most common variants in use on both sides.

Top: Abandoned *Khosta* of the 21st Independent Motor-Rifle Brigade captured by Ukrainian forces in Nizhyn, March 2022. The 120mm 2A80 rifled mortar has a distinctive profile and muzzle brake. Bottom: Russian modernised *Gvozdika* (2S1M1) battery during exercises in the Eastern Military District, September 2012. The characteristic SNS antenna is visible between the gun and PG-2 panoramic sight. (ZSU; MORF)

Technical Summary

The *Gvozdika*'s 122mm D-32 howitzer is essentially identical to the D-30A, with minor modifications to adapt it to the more confined environment of an SPG such as the fume extractor. The howitzer can also be elevated up to 70°. As with the *Akatsiya*, the *Gvozdika* turret employs an electromechanical elevation/traverse drive and has 360° traverse for rapid reaction all-round fire capability. Indirect fire aiming is done with the gunner's PG-2 panoramic periscopic sight, while direct fire is conducted using the OP5-37 telescopic sight. Unlike on the *Akatsiya*, there is no self-defence machine gun for the commander. The communications suite of Soviet-legacy *Gvozdikas* is the same as on *Akatsiya*, consisting of the *Magnolia*-M radio and *Lebed* crew intercom.

Loading is done with the assistance of a rammer, allowing for a maximum aimed rate-of-fire of 4–5 rounds/minute according to the technical description. The rammer is attached to the gun and can load it at any elevation angle. The *Gvozdika* carries a total of 40 rounds (projectile + charge) onboard, of which 24 are in the turret's ready racks and another 16 in the rear hull. There is no mechanised ammunition rack like on the *Akatsiya*. Firing using the rear hull racks cuts the rate-of-fire to 1.5–2 rounds/minute. *Gvozdikas* may also be supplied with ammunition externally via the rear door if firing from fixed positions, which allows them to sustain a higher rate-of-fire. To assist with this, a sliding conveyor chute can be set up in the rear hull; there is no motor, it is gravity-powered.

In order to minimise weight, the *Gvozdika*'s armour is thinner than the *Akatsiya*'s, with a maximum thickness of 20mm on the turret front, 15mm on the hull front.[23] The rest of the armour (7mm thick) is intended to protect the crew of four against small arms fire (7.62mm B-32 AP bullets from 300m) from all angles, but not much else.[24] [25] Like on the *Akatsiya*, a positive pressure ventilation system is installed to reduce gun gas contamination in the fighting compartment during extended periods of firing, as well as providing nuclear, biological, and chemical (NBC) protection. It takes no more than two minutes to emplace/displace the *Gvozdika*.

Automotively, the *Gvozdika* chassis is derived from the MT-LB via the stretched MT-LBu. Known simply as the '*universalnoye gusenichnoye lyogkoye shassi*' ('universal tracked light chassis') in the manual, it is powered by the same 300hp YaMZ-238N supercharged four-stroke V-8 diesel engine found in the MT-LBu. At a fully loaded weight of 15.7t, this provides the *Gvozdika* a respectable power/weight ratio of ~19hp/t. The mechanical two-flow transmission with planetary-friction steering mechanisms has six forward and one reverse gears, allowing for a maximum road speed of 60km/h and reverse speed of 6km/h. The *Gvozdika*, like the rest of the MT-LB family, can also neutral-steer. The engine and transmission are both front-mounted, with the driver sitting to the left of the engine compartment, behind the transmission.

The *Gvozdika* is blessed with excellent cross-country and rough terrain capabilities, which it inherited from the MT-LB. It uses a torsion bar suspension with seven road wheels and single-pin 'live' tracks. The first and last torsion bar units on each side also have a telescoping hydraulic shock absorber. Because of its light weight, the *Gvozdika* has an average specific ground pressure of only 48.2kPa, 18 percent lower than its 152mm counterpart, the *Akatsiya* (58.8kPa). This low ground pressure allowed it to better negotiate mud or sand that would otherwise be impassable to heavier SPGs.

In addition to its good cross-country capabilities, like the MT-LB, the *Gvozdika* is amphibious with minimal preparations. Once in the water, it is propelled by its tracks, aided by mounted grilles to properly redirect water flow from the tracks, to a maximum speed of 4.5km/h. This form of propulsion is sufficient in relatively calm river crossings, but is insufficient for naval landings except in all but the calmest seas. Soviet offensive doctrine at the time preferred as many of the combat vehicles to have amphibious capability as possible, as reflected in the BMP-1 infantry fighting vehicle (IFV) and BTR-60 APC; this would theoretically allow them to retain offensive momentum while crossing the many rivers that criss-cross Europe and reduce the traffic bottlenecks created by bridges or river fords.

Ukrainian *Gvozdika* of the 92nd 'Ivan Sirko' Mechanised (now Assault) Brigade firing during exercises, 2016. (92 Assault)

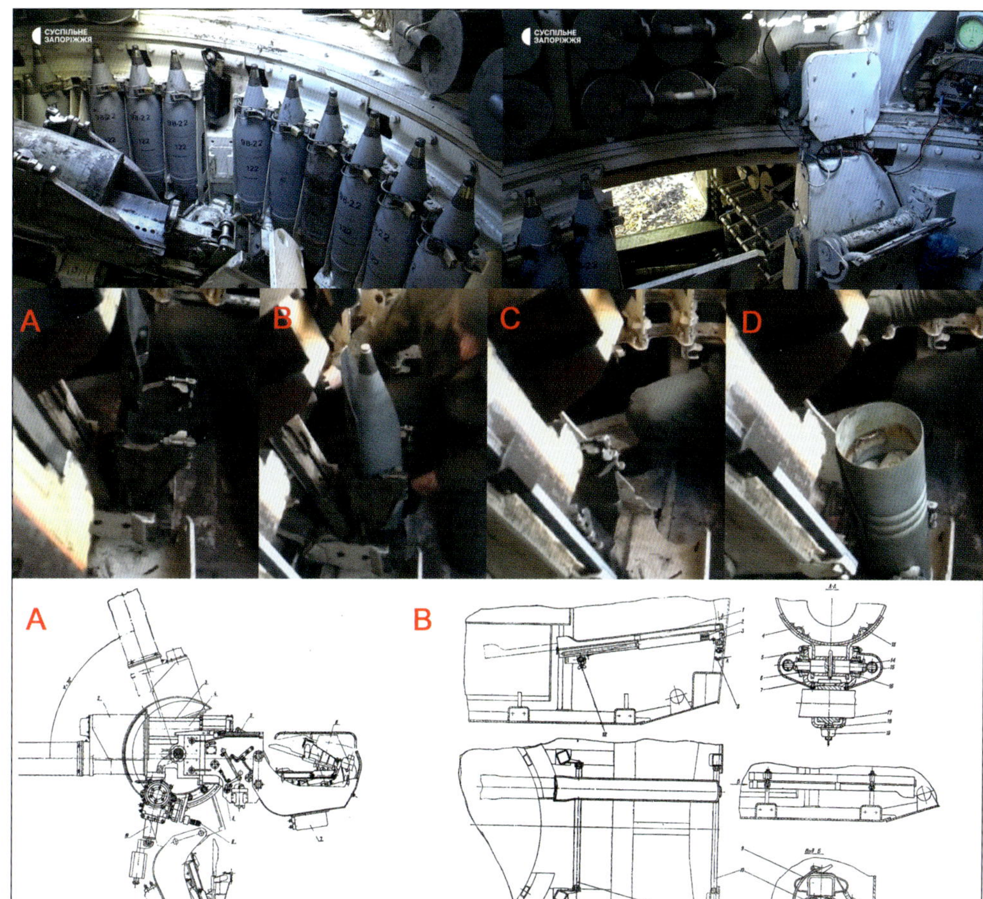

Top: ammunition stowage onboard a *Gvozdika*. Projectiles are stored below the turret ring while charges are stored in the turret bustle and right turret wall. There is further stowage behind the turret in the hull, and the rear hull door can be used to pass ammunition in. Middle: loading with the rammer (A). The loader places the projectile in the rammer's tray before pushing it to align with the breech (B), causing it to automatically ram the shell in (C). The loader next places the charge in the tray (D), then rams it in by pressing a button, which also causes the rammer to return to its original position after it is done. Bottom: illustrations of the rammer (A) and conveyor chute (B) for externally supplied ammunition. (Suspilne Zaporizhzhia; YouTube; author's collection)

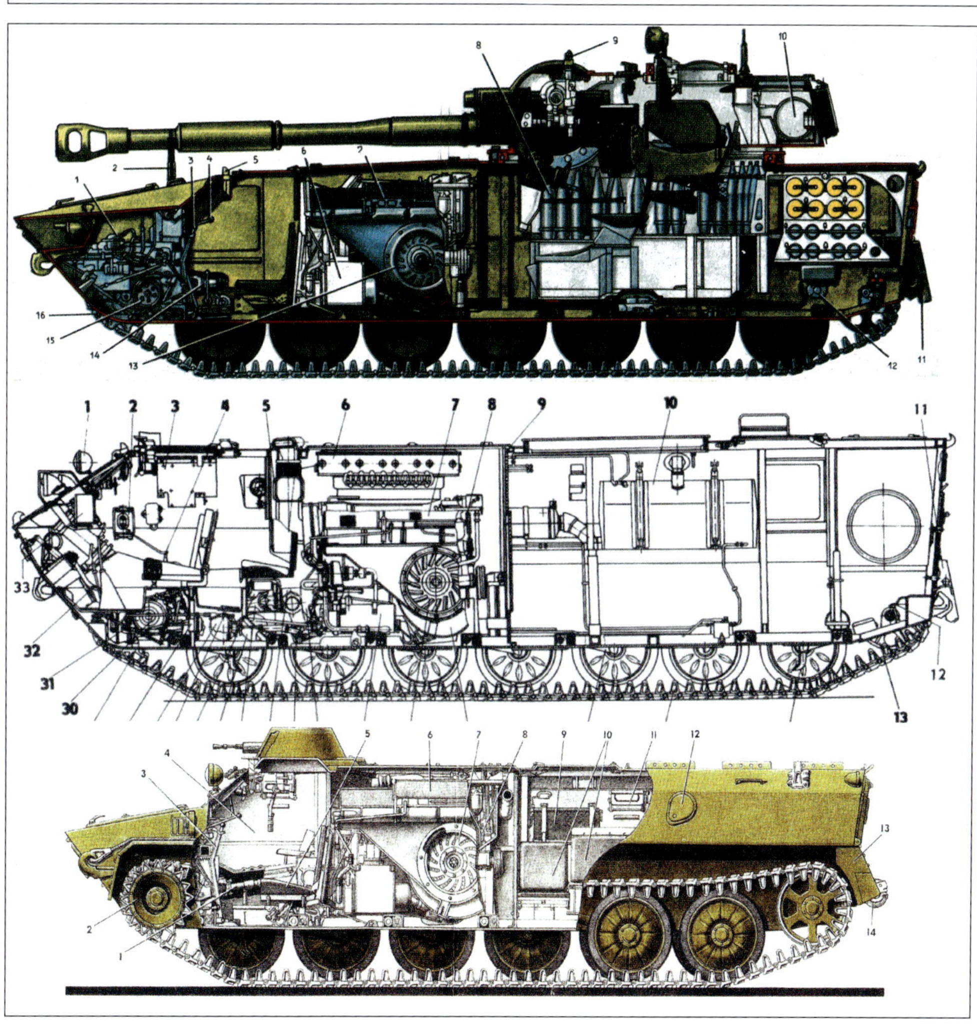

Cutaways of the *Gvozdika*, MT-LBu, and MT-LB, from Soviet military posters and manuals, illustrating their automotive and layout similarities. (Author's collection)

Ukrainian *Gvozdika* of the 72nd 'Black Zaporizhzhians' Mechanised Brigade demonstrates its amphibious capabilities during an exercise at the Shirokyi Lan training grounds, September 2016. This capability has seen very little (if any) use on both sides throughout the war. Inset: manual illustration showing the trim vane and grilles set up before amphibious operations. (ZSU; author's collection)

VDV D-30A in action on the Sievierodonetsk front, May 2022. The VDV were among the few VSRF units to retain the D-30 in active service at the beginning of the 2022 invasion due to its air transportability. (MORF)

Context

During the Cold War, the D-30 served as both the standard Soviet divisional and regimental artillery, mostly replacing the M-30 howitzer and various 76mm field pieces like the ZIS-3. It provided a significant increase in firepower for Soviet tank and motor-rifle divisions, and was also the heaviest indirect fire support that could be dropped with the VDV during airborne operations.[26] Similarly, the *Gvozdika* would in turn mostly replace the D-30 and M-30 at the regimental level for tank and motor-rifle divisions as the emphasis shifted towards SPGs for their greater perceived survivability and mobility to keep up with advancing mechanised forces.[27] The 122mm pieces perform a role analogous to 105mm pieces within NATO forces, acting in direct support of their constituent regiments. They are, however, generally heavier and hit harder than 105mm pieces by virtue of firing a heavier shell with more explosive filler. NATO also currently does not operate a 105mm SPG since the British Abbot was retired in the 1990s.

The period leading up to the Russo-Ukrainian War may have seemed like the twilight years of the 122mm calibre in both Russian and Ukrainian service. In 2012, the VSRF had 564 active D-30As in service, but in February 2013, Russian Minister of Defence Sergey Shoigu had announced the removal of all D-30As from active Russian Army units, to be placed in storage, and their place would be taken by *Msta*-B towed guns or the *Akatsiya*. Only the VDV would officially retain the D-30A in service, although a few other units maintained them as late as 2020. *Gvozdika*s were still kept in service with the VSRF prior to 2022, but their active numbers were relatively small: estimated at approximately 622 across 20 units in 2012, outnumbered by 152mm SPGs by about 2.6:1.[28] It was planned to be replaced by the *Khosta*, but this was not close to being achieved before the Russian full-scale invasion in February 2022. D-30s and Gvozdikas were also used by the Luhansk/Donetsk militias, some probably captured from Ukrainian storage bases, but most were likely sent by Russia from storage.

Similarly, the Ukrainian Ministry of Defence had decided to retire all its *Gvozdikas* (it had inherited 563 from the USSR) in 2013 due to 'changes in military doctrine'. At the start of the Donbas War in 2014, some brigades had already disbanded their *Gvozdika* units, while others were in the process of doing so. The outbreak of war led to a hasty reversal of this decision, and the *Gvozdikas* have remained an essential part of the Ukrainian artillery ever since.[29] In 2016 it was reported that modernisation efforts had begun on the *Gvozdika*, which included the incorporation of digital radios, domestic SNS for navigation, and replacement of the YaMZ engine with a more modern Volvo diesel engine.[30] The author has not been able to find out how many, if any, of the Ukrainian *Gvozdikas* have been modernised in this way. Because the *Gvozdika* and MT-LB were made in Kharkiv, it is likely that they are the easiest Soviet era SPGs for Ukraine to support logistically, especially after D-30/2A31 barrel production was mastered in Kramatorsk in 2020.[31] Ukraine also inherited 531 D-30s, but they remained in service only with Ukrainian paratroopers, internal troops and coastal defence troops by 2014, with a significant number (91) exported overseas. After 2014, many were brought out of storage, particularly to arm the newly established NHU. The role that the D-30 plays as a training gun should also not be underestimated: as Zhirokhov notes, due to plentiful 122mm ammunition allowing gunnery practice using the D-30, the artillery arm was one of the relatively few parts of the ZSU that was not left to rot completely from 1991–2014. It continued to serve in this role in the period leading up to 2022, regularly taking part in exercises and allowing ZSU artillery gunners to hone their skills in conjunction with American AN/TPQ-36 and AN/TPQ-37 Firefinder counterbattery radars and brigade-level UASs.[32] These skills would serve them well during the 2022 invasion.

Both the *Gvozdika* and D-30 have proven themselves to be effective and well-liked weapons over their decades of service. However, it remains to be seen if they will have a postwar future in both countries: whether Ukraine chooses to switch completely to NATO 105mm and 155mm calibres, and whether Russia will continue its plans to replace the 122mm with 120mm rifled mortars. With the war going on, though, it is safe to say that as long as 122mm ammunition and barrels are still available, the D-30 and *Gvozdika* will not be going away any time soon.

Ukrainian *Gvozdika* fires at a target, September 2023. Alongside *Akatsiya*, *Gvozdika* was numerically the most important Ukrainian SPG at the start of the 2022 invasion. (ZSU General Staff)

RAPIRA: REPURPOSED BLADE

Entering service in 1961, the T-12 (GRAU: 2A19) was the first smoothbore AT gun in the world to enter service, predating the T-62 main battle tank (MBT) by several years. Using newly developed APFSDS (armour-piercing fin-stabilised discarding sabot) rounds fired from its 100mm L/73 barrel, the T-12 could deal with any contemporary MBT frontally without requiring exceptionally powerful charges and the bulk needed to withstand such forces: a combat weight of only ~3t, 1.3t lighter than the Second World War German 8.8cm Pak 43/41. The improved MT-12 (GRAU: 2A29) soon followed in 1970. Sometimes referred to as '*Rapira*' ('Rapier'), the T-12/MT-12 family were considered useful as a cheaper supplement to sophisticated anti-tank guided missiles (ATGMs) such as *Malyutka* that could also cover some of their limitations (high minimum engagement range, low rate-of-fire, long engagement times, and high operator skill requirements). In addition to the AT role, *Rapiras* had a useful indirect-fire capability as it was able to fire the 16.7kg 3OF35 HE-Frag shell at 700m/s, although the 20° maximum elevation limited its range to only 8.2km without creative measures.[33]

Unlike NATO, the USSR never completely abandoned towed AT guns. Throughout the Cold War, it invested in modernising the *Rapira* family with such innovations as the radar-based *Ruta* (1A31) FCS for the MT-12R (2A29R) variant to provide all-weather capability or the laser-guided 9M117 ATGM integrated onboard the MT-12K (2A29K) variant as a part of the *Kastet* (9K116) system. Both Russia (468 in service 2013) and Ukraine (120 in 2012) have inherited significant quantities of these guns and their ammunition.[34] They are obsolete against modern MBTs' frontal protection, but still nominally served as direct-fire AT guns in both armies up till the early stages of the 2022 invasion. While ATGMs have mostly supplanted them in AT units, *Rapiras* continue to perform a valuable role as training guns and are also used as indirect fire weapons, with both the Ukrainians and Russians even sometimes mounting the guns on MT-LBs as *ersatz* SPGs.[35] [36] It is hard to imagine the *Rapira* being used often in its originally envisaged tank destroyer role at this stage of the war, but the relatively static nature of the fighting and the *Rapira*'s respectable indirect fire capabilities have allowed it to stay useful.

Rapira (MT-12) of 55 Art. Note the distinctive integral honeycomb muzzle brake. Each Ukrainian artillery brigade nominally had an AT artillery battalion with *Rapira* AT guns, but they have now mostly been replaced in this role by ATGMs. (55 Art.)

4
TYULPAN: MORTAR COMBAT

Development History

Modern smoothbore mortars, consisting of a tube with a firing pin and baseplate at one end firing low-velocity fin-stabilised mortar bombs, were first introduced during the First World War. They are lighter, much simpler and cheaper than comparable rifled guns, being no more than steel pipes attached to metal plates at the end. The impulse acting on the bomb during firing is much lower due to the smaller propelling charge used, allowing for thinner projectile walls and more explosive filler, and the lower velocity also allows such bombs to be fired in high arcs, dropping almost vertically on top of a target. However, mortars have much shorter ranges than conventional artillery, and usually cannot be used for direct fire since they have no recoil mechanisms and must be fired at high elevations for the baseplate to work.[1]

The Soviets were quite keen on these weapons, and by 1938, the SKB-4 design bureau in Leningrad under Boris Shavyrin had developed a system of 50–120mm muzzle-loading smoothbore mortars. It included the 120mm *obr.* 1938 *g.* (PM-38) regimental mortar, which had impressed the Germans enough that they copied it (with minor modifications) as the 12cm GrW 42.[2] In order to partially make up for their inferiority in conventional artillery during much of the Second World War, the Soviets would end up relying heavily on these mortars. To get some idea, in 1943 the Soviets fired over twice as many mortar bombs at the Germans than vice versa: 10.8 million of these were 120mm mortar bombs, about twice the number of 122mm M-30 howitzer shells expended over the same period.[3]

Still, as early as 1938 the Soviets saw the need for heavier mortars, and had already issued a requirement for 160mm and 240mm mortars. This need became more apparent after the Winter War against Finland: at a secret meeting held in April 1940 discussing experience gained from the Winter War, Stalin himself remarked that 'all corps, all companies, battalions, and regiments must have 6-inch (152mm) mortars, 8-inch (203mm) mortars. This is terribly necessary for modern warfare'. He would go on to say 'A mortar is a wonderful thing…if you want to have a war with little blood, do not spare the mortar bombs'.[4]

Unfortunately, the German invasion in 1941 meant that the first heavy mortar, the 160mm *obr.* 1943 *g.* (MT-13), would not enter service until 1944 as the Soviet arms industry prioritised existing weapons. That same year, Shavryn's team was tasked with designing a 240mm 'high-power' ('*bolshoy moshchnosti*') mortar, which eventually entered service in 1950 while series production began at *Zavod* 75, Yurga, in 1951.[5] [6] This was the 240mm M-240, a massive 4.1t breech-loading weapon that stood over 5.3m tall with its barrel at the maximum 80° elevation. It could hurl a 131kg F-864 HE mortar bomb at a muzzle velocity of 362m/s out to 9.7km with maximum charges. However, it was also a most cumbersome piece, rated to take 20–25 minutes to emplace and 15–20 minutes to displace.[7]

By the 1960s, this was far too slow for the modern battlefield, especially with the M-240's short range. Thus, development of an SP version codenamed '*Tyulpan*' ('Tulip'; GRAU: 2S4) began contemporaneously with the *Akatsiya* and *Gvozdika*.[8] As with the *Gvozdika*, the BMP-1, MT-LB, and Object 123/124 were considered

Russian *Tyulpan* of the Southern Military District during exercises in the Tarskoye mountain range, North Ossetia, January 2022. The *Tyulpan* is a very unique and specialised artillery piece with no equivalent in Western artillery arsenals. (MORF)

120mm *obr.* 1938 *g.* regimental mortar in service with the so-called Donetsk People's Republic's 1st 'Sloviansk' Brigade during exercises, January 2016. Weighing only around 250kg, this Second World War veteran is capable of throwing a 16kg bomb nearly 6km. (Gennadiy Dubovoy)

Left: illustration of the M-240 from the manual. Right: Ukrainian M-240 in service with the 3rd Assault Brigade; this weapon was not in Ukrainian service prior to 2022. To reload, the barrel is depressed (inset), almost like a break action shotgun, and one of the massive bombs is lifted to the breech. (Author's collection; ArmyTV)

as the base. The latter was chosen, and development of the chassis took place simultaneously with the *Akatsiya* at Yefimov's OKB-3, while adapting the M-240 for the *Tyulpan* fell to Yuri Kalachnikov's team at OKB-172.[9] Testing was completed in 1971 and the *Tyulpan* entered service in 1972.[10] Relatively few were built (probably ~500 by the time production ceased in 1987), due to the relatively specialised nature of the weapon as well as its high cost: a *Tyulpan* in 1972 cost over five times more than an *Akatsiya* (₽210,000 vs. ₽36,500).[11] [12]

Technical Summary

The sole reason for the *Tyulpan*'s existence is to transport and deploy its 240mm 2B8 smoothbore mortar within range of enemy positions. The 2B8 is ballistically identical to the M-240 and shares the same ammunition. However, the key difference is that a lot of the processes have been mechanised on the *Tyulpan*. The 2B8 is transported horizontally on top; in combat, it is erected into position facing the *Tyulpan*'s rear by hydraulic mechanisms, with the massive hexagonal baseplate supporting the rear of the vehicle for stability. The elevation ranges from 50° to 80°; due to the way the mortar must pivot on the baseplate and safety reasons, the traverse arc varies depending on the elevation: from +/-41° at 80° to +/-10° at 50°.[13] It takes 'only' five minutes to emplace the *Tyulpan*, and 10 minutes to displace it, roughly half those of the M-240.[14]

The *Tyulpan* can carry up to 20 HE mortar bombs or 10 RAPs within the vehicle in a mechanised rotary magazine (one RAP takes up the space of two HE bombs). The loading process is heavily automated with a mechanical rammer, but the *Tyulpan*'s rate-of-fire is only ~0.9 rounds/minute since the crew has to exit the vehicle in order to prepare the heavy rounds for firing by attaching the primary and secondary charges by hand. Like all Soviet SPGs, the *Tyulpan* can also operate using solely externally supplied ammunition, for which a small crane is provided on the vehicle to help with handling the 130kg bombs (or 228kg RAPs). Aiming is done manually with the MP-46M panoramic sight attached to the mortar mount: the gunner must exit the vehicle to aim the mortar with it. There is no provision for direct fire.[15]

The 1984 standard communications suite consists of the *Magnolia*-M radio and *Lebed* crew intercom. From late 2017, Russian *Tyulpans* undergoing overhaul began receiving upgrades to their fire control, communications, and navigation systems. It has not been specified exactly how they have been upgraded, though it can be safely assumed that it involves replacing the old Soviet radios with modern ones like *Akveduk* and adding an SNS, allowing them to be integrated into ESU TZ.[16, 17] A variant of the *Mekhanizator* receiver, 1V522, was developed for *Tyulpans* in the 1980s, but it never entered service: it is unknown whether this is being implemented now or if a completely new system has been developed.[18]

'*Tyulpantik*' operating near Rubizhne, May 2022. It was filmed by Russian journalist Aleksandr Kots and subsequently destroyed by Ukrainian counterbattery fire the next day after its position was reportedly geolocated using the video this still was taken from. The mortar's high arc trajectories mean that buildings are rarely an obstacle for the *Tyulpan*, making it a powerful weapon in urban combat. (Aleksandr Kots)

Tyulpan in its traveling (left) and deployed (right) configurations. The crew must exit the vehicle in order to aim, load, and fire the 2B8 mortar. (MORF)

The chassis used by the *Tyulpan* is more or less automotively identical to that of the *Akatsiya*: the reader is invited to refer to that section for details. The *Tyulpan* is somewhat heavier than the *Akatsiya*, at 30t, though once undeployed its mobility characteristics are pretty similar. Its hull armour is also identical to the *Akatsiya*'s. The vehicle only has room for two of the five crewmembers, the driver and commander: the latter has his own cupola, with a remotely-operated PKT AAMG mount (1,500 rounds provided) similar to that on the *Akatsiya*. The remaining crewmembers must either ride externally on the vehicle or in an accompanying APC. It also retains the manually-operated dozer blade for digging emplacements.

Context

In terms of raw explosive power, the *Tyulpan* is undoubtedly the most powerful artillery gun currently deployed by any nation. The only artillery piece in service to match that calibre is the 240mm

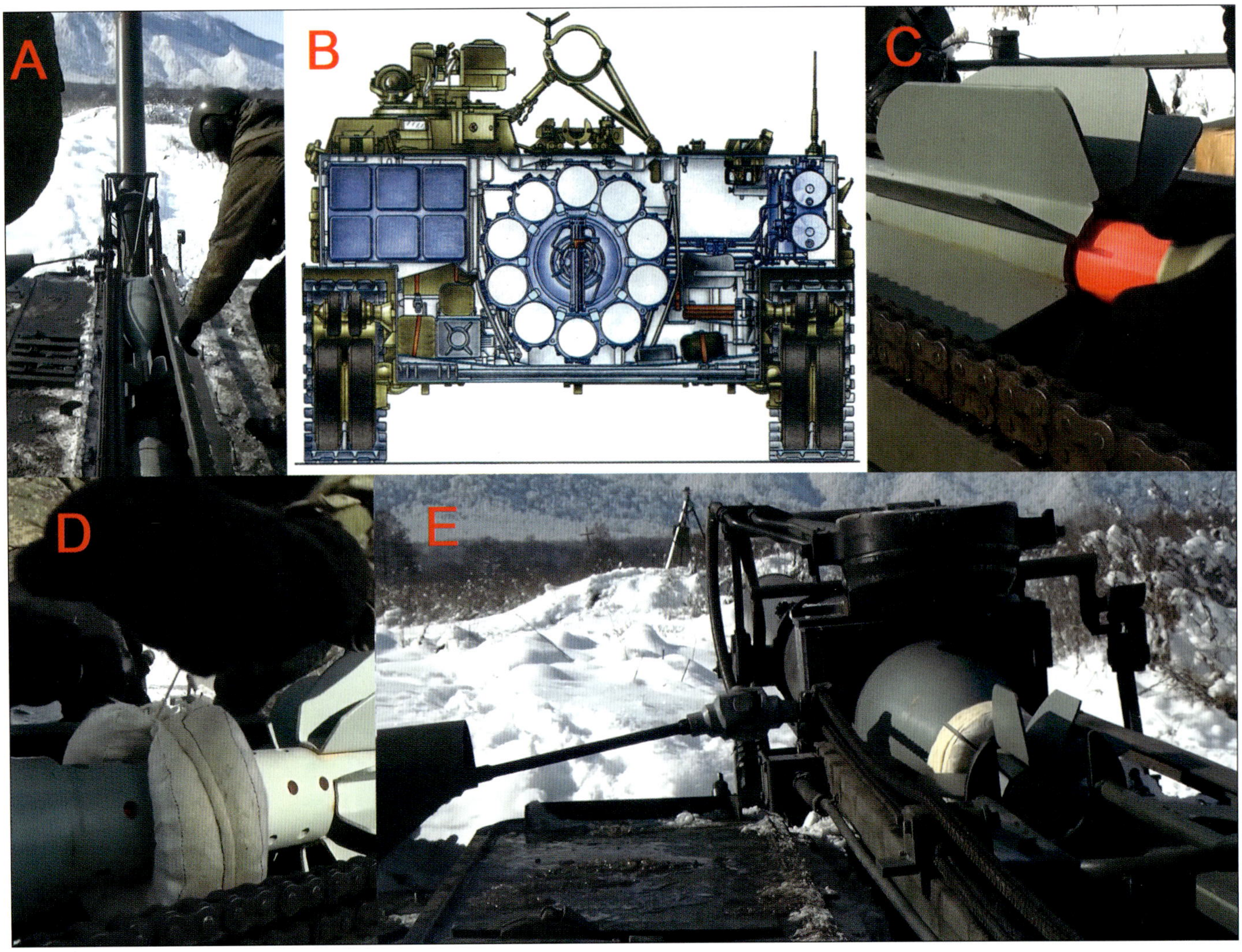

Loading process: first, a bomb is brought up (A) from the rotary magazine (B). The primary charge is inserted (C), with additional bagged charges tied as needed (D). The barrel is then depressed to the loading line and the complete round is rammed into the breech (E). Once loaded, the round breech block with obturator is automatically lowered and locked, and the mortar is elevated to the firing position. (MORF)

Tyulpan of the Western Military District moving to a firing position, August 2022. (MORF)

Howitzer M1, which is only used by the Republic of China (ROC) on its Kinmen and Matsu islands' coastal batteries: however, even though the shell it fires is heavier (160kg), it has less explosive filler (22kg).[19] The 2B8 mortar's high-arcing trajectory results in the bomb dropping near vertically on top of targets, often the weakest part of a fortification and optimal for fragment dispersal. The *Smelchak* (1K113) laser-guided PGM complex, with the assistance of a laser-equipped forward observer or UAS, also enables it to be accurately hit point targets, with a hit probability of 80–90 percent within a circle of 2–3m diameter.[20]

Soviet *Tyulpans* were usually organised into heavy SP mortar brigades that formed part of the ARVGK, where it served alongside the M-240. These units, directly subordinated to the High Command (GK – *Glavkom*), would be committed at critical points to support units that needed firepower beyond what their organic 122/152mm assets could provide.[21] Unlike other Soviet artillery pieces, nearly all *Tyulpans* have been inherited by Russia since 1991. Twenty-five were known to have been in service in 2000, eight of which were in the 45th High-Power Artillery Brigade, which is directly subordinate to the Western Military District in a similar manner to Soviet ARVGK units. The type had actually been retired in 2009 along with the brigade's disbandment, but both were brought back into service in 2017 as part of the MORF's large-scale reform significantly reinforcing the VSRF's artillery units.[22] There is no evidence Ukraine inherited any post-1991.

For all its power, the *Tyulpan* also has some very serious limitations. The most serious of these is range: even with the 3F2 *Gargara* RAP, the maximum range is only 20km, well within reach of modern NATO 155mm pieces. On the modern battlefield where accurate and rapid counterbattery fire is common, along with the emerging threat of loitering munitions, this imposes severe restrictions on *Tyulpan* employment. This is not helped by the relatively long emplacement/displacement time as well. Against the less well-equipped Afghan *mujahideen* or Chechen fighters the *Tyulpan* faced previously, these limitations were not as apparent. However, the Ukrainian military is a very different proposition, and this is reflected by the losses suffered so far by the *Tyulpan* fleet in Ukraine (at least 52 as of October 2024, high considering the small number thought to be in service).

Having said that, if employed correctly and protected with the right support, the *Tyulpan* is a devastating weapon against fortifications and other strongpoints. During the siege of Mariupol, a *Tyulpan* battery was reportedly able to collapse a nine-storey apartment building, and they were also used to bombard the Ukrainian defenders making their last stand at the Azovstal steel factory.[23] As the defenders lacked air support and the ability to effectively counterbattery the *Tyulpans*, this battle represents a near-ideal environment for the *Tyulpan* to operate in.

5
GIATSINT: A CLASS OF ITS OWN

Development History

From the 1950s to the 1970s, the primary Soviet long-range gun was the 130mm M-46 corps field gun. The M-46 had outstanding range for its time: 27.5km with 33kg 3OF3 HE-Frag at 930m/s, easily outranging contemporary NATO 105mm and 155mm pieces, as US forces would experience firsthand in Vietnam. This was achieved via the use of a very long L/55 barrel and powerful charge (the complete round (projectile and full charge) weighed 59.1kg, nearly as much as that for the 152mm D-20). The trade-off was a rather heavy gun (7.7t) for the projectile fired, but the long range meant the reduced mobility was acceptable.[1]

However, as early as 1958 it became apparent that a longer ranged gun firing a heavier shell was desirable. During the Second Taiwan Strait crisis, PLA M-46s duelled with ROC 240mm Howitzer M1s based on the Kinmen and Matsu islands. The M-46s found themselves unable to match the range of the ROC howitzers without resorting to warming up the charges and firing with a tailwind. In addition, the relatively light 130mm shells were ineffective against the hardened bunkers the ROC had constructed to house the howitzers.[2] By the late 1960s, the American 175mm Self-Propelled Field Artillery Gun M107 had also entered service and was being used in combat in Vietnam. Its 175mm M113 gun was capable of firing a 65kg M437 HE-Frag projectile at 914m/s to nearly 33km; not only did it outrange any Soviet piece (though its long L/60 barrel suffered from high barrel wear), but as an SPG it was also far quicker to displace and more difficult to catch with counterbattery fire.[3 4]

Nuclear warhead design had also improved enough to make nuclear artillery shells a reality, but the 130mm calibre was too small. In light of all these events, the Soviets began developing a range of new nuclear-capable long-range guns, one of which was a 152mm gun that would come in both SP and towed forms. The project was formally authorised in 1970 under the name *Giatsint* ('Hyacinth'). Previously, the Soviets would take an already established towed gun and use it for an SPG; now, development of the towed (*Giatsint*-B) and SP (*Giatsint*-S) guns, as well as their ammunition, would occur simultaneously.[5]

Giatsint-B (GRAU: 2A36) and *Giatsint*-S's armament (GRAU: 2A37) was assigned to Motovilikha's OKB-172 under Kalachnikov's leadership. The first ballistic test models were completed in time for testing in 1971. The muzzle blast was found to be excessive (even by Soviet standards), and the gun was modified with a lengthened barrel and reduced full charge. While OKB-172 was developing the gun, Uraltransmash's OKB-3 under Yefimov was assigned the chassis for the *Giatsint*-S (GRAU: 2S5; GBTU: 307). Yefimov's team would once again use the proven Object 123/124 as the basis for the *Giatsint*-S; in fact, many parts would be derived from the *Akatsiya* and *Tyulpan* to simplify development. However, the programme was delayed by problems, especially with the new 152mm ammunition. Eventually, after more extensive testing, both *Giatsints* were accepted into service around the end of 1978.[6]

Giatsints would replace the venerable M-46/47 at the army/corps level within the 1980s Soviet Army, particularly within forces stationed west of the Urals and in Eastern Europe.[7] However, they were never exported to the Warsaw Pact or widely abroad the way the M-46 was, even after the USSR's collapse. One of the few countries to operate both types was Finland, and it has sent some retired *Giatsint*-Bs as aid to Ukraine.[8] It is known that Motovilikha built 1,255 *Giatsint*-Bs and another 1,255 2A37 guns for the *Giatsint*-S before production ceased in 1991, though the actual number of SPGs is thought to be lower (~975).[9] Since 1991 there have been several proposed upgrades for *Giatsints* in Russian service, but these have not been adopted.[10] It is thus reasonable to assume that *Giatsints* being used by both sides in the Russo-Ukrainian War do not differ dramatically from the 1980s descriptions of the systems provided in the following technical summaries.

Left: Ex-Finnish 152mm *Giatsint*-B (152 K 89) in Ukrainian service with distinctive two-tone green camouflage. The author's NHU acquaintance has personal experience operating the gun: 'typically Soviet: unpleasant and physically demanding to operate, but virtually unbreakable'. Right: *Giatsint*-S of 26 Art., July 2020. This was the only ZSU brigade to operate *Giatsint*-Ss prior to the 2022 invasion. (ArmySOS; 26 Art.)

Ukrainian Marines' D-20, 406th Artillery Brigade, with pixel camouflage seen during the *Shtorm*-2018 combined exercise, August 2018. Prior to 2014, 406 Art. was a coastal artillery unit based in Crimea; roughly half the unit's officers (including the commanding officer) defected to Russia after the Crimean annexation. (Artwork by David Bocquelet)

Ukrainian *Akatsiya* (2S3M), 92nd Assault Brigade, October 2023. Originally a mechanised brigade, it was redesignated an assault brigade in August 2023. The brigade's field insignia can be seen on the turret. (Artwork by David Bocquelet)

Russian *Akatsiya* (2S3M2) 'Kuban', unidentified unit, November 2022. The 2S3M2 upgrade introduced the SNS antenna behind the commander's cupola. The slogan '*OPKhZ-33 sila*' ('Power to OPKhZ-33') appears to refer to the Soviet 33rd NBC Defence Rgt. of the Pacific Fleet, suggesting it is from one of their units. (Artwork by David Bocquelet)

Ukrainian D-30A 'Valter', NHU Azov Special Purpose Unit, ca. 2016. Azov started off as a volunteer militia battalion in spring 2014 before being turned into an NHU regiment in the fall, whereupon it received D-30s. It is now a brigade (12th Special Purpose Brigade) of the Ukrainian Offensive Guard. (Artwork by David Bocquelet)

Russian *Gvozdika* No. 634 of the so-called 'Donetsk People's Republic', August 2022. The slogan says 'To Kiev'. *Gvozdikas* were used by the Donetsk and Luhansk militias during both the Donbas War and the 2022 Russian invasion. (Artwork by David Bocquelet)

Ukrainian *Gvozdika*, 92nd Mechanised Brigade, ca. 2014. During the Donbas War, 92 Mech.'s *Gvozdikas* fought as an incomplete artillery division of five SPGs, the remaining seven being transferred to other units. (Artwork by David Bocquelet)

Ukrainian *Giatsint*-B, unidentified unit, June 2015. Ukraine inherited considerably more towed *Giatsint*-Bs than SP *Giatsint*-Ss; however, only 406 Art. had these powerful pieces in service at the start of the Russo-Ukrainian War. (Artwork by David Bocquelet)

Russian *Giatsint*-S 'Snayper', unidentified unit, June 2022. Russian *Giatsint*-Ss have generally not received the level of upgrades that *Msta*-Ss or *Akatsiyas* have, and they are relatively uncommon in service. (Artwork by David Bocquelet)

Russian *Tyulpan* 'Batyr', unidentified unit, May 2023. These powerful but rare SP mortars are used sparingly due to their relatively inflexible nature of deployment and vulnerability to counterbattery fire or UASs. (Artwork by David Bocquelet)

Russian *Msta*-B 'Pchelka', unidentified unit, July 2022. *Msta*-Bs were the most common towed 152mm pieces used by both sides at the start of the Russo-Ukrainian War. (Artwork by David Bocquelet)

Ukrainian *Msta*-S, 26th Artillery Brigade, summer 2014. This was the only Ukrainian unit to use *Msta*-Ss from 2014 until the 2022 Russian invasion. (Artwork by David Bocquelet)

Russian *Msta*-SM2 No. 621, 205th Motor-Rifle Brigade, February 2023. This unit is based in the Caucasus (Stavropol Krai) and has participated in every conflict Russia has been involved in since 1991. (Artwork by David Bocquelet)

Ukrainian *Pion*, 43rd Artillery Brigade, July 2024. The white triangle on green background is the tactical symbol used by Ukrainian forces during the 2024 Ukrainian invasion of Russia in Kursk *oblast*. (Artwork by David Bocquelet)

Russian *Pion* 'King Kong', unidentified unit, October 2022. 'N-2200' is an index assigned by the Russian railway system to oversized (*negabaritnost*) railway cargo, with each number indicating the degree of oversize in each zone (lower, lateral, upper, and vertical). (Artwork by David Bocquelet)

Russian *Malva*, unidentified unit, July 2024. One of the newest Russian artillery systems, this *Malva* was operating in the Belgorod *oblast* when it was hit and damaged by tungsten balls from an M30A1 PFF rocket fired by a Ukrainian HIMARS/MLRS. (Artwork by David Bocquelet)

Russian *Nona*-S No. 466, 331st VDV Rgt., November 2022, destroyed near Nova Kakhovka, Kherson *oblast*. It bore the name 'Fury' on its lower glacis; the American Second World War movie 'Fury' about an M4A2(76) HVSS tank crew is popular on both sides of the war among tank and AFV crews. (Artwork by David Bocquelet)

Russian *Nona*-SVK, unidentified unit, February 2023. Only two Russian units were known to use *Nona*-SVKs in 2018: the 55th Guards Mountain Motor-Rifle Brigade and the 752nd Motor-Rifle Regiment. (Artwork by David Bocquelet)

Ukrainian 1V13, 26th Artillery Brigade, December 2020. 1V13/1V13Ms are the battery senior officer vehicles of the Soviet 1V12/1V12M *Mashina/Faltset* complex, directly responsible for relaying commands and targeting information vertically from command vehicles to SPG batteries. (Artwork by David Bocquelet)

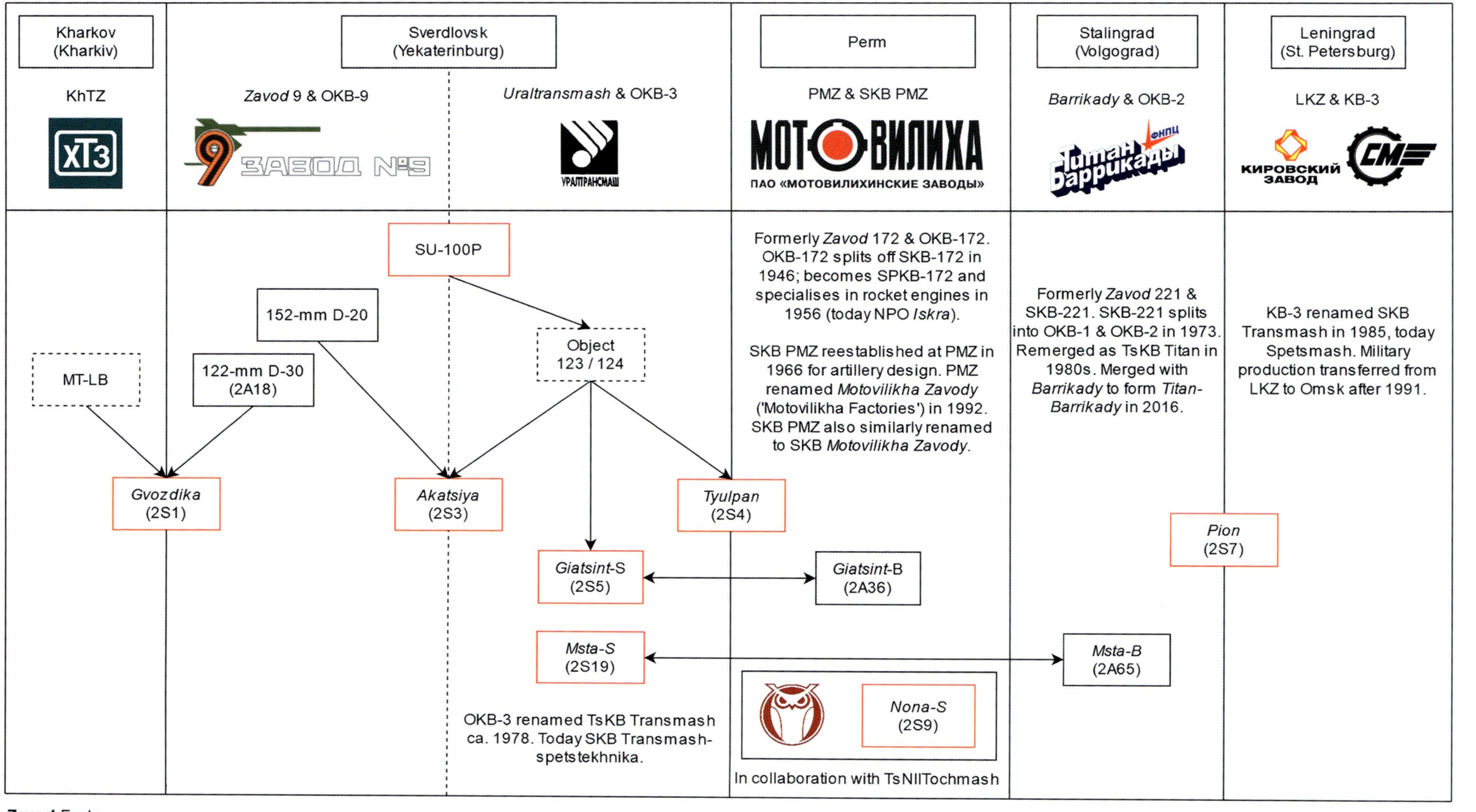

Zavod: Factory
OKB: *opytno konstruktorskoye byuro* ('experimental design bureau'); **TsKB**: *tsentralno KB* ('central design bureau'); **SKB**: *spetsialno KB* ('special design bureau').
KhTZ: *Kharkivskyi traktornyi zavod* ('Kharkiv Tractor Factory', in Ukrainian).
Uraltransmash: *Uralskiy zavod transportnogo mashinostroeniya* ('Ural Transport Engineering Factory').
PMZ: *Permskiy mashinostroitelniy zavod* ('Perm Machine-building Factory').
TsNIITochmash: *Tsentralniy nauchno-issledovatelskiy institut tochnogo mashinostroeniya* ('Central Research Institute for Precision Engineering').
LKZ: *Leningrad Kirovskiy zavod* ('Leningrad Kirov Factory').

'Family tree' of Soviet artillery designs, their design bureaux and associated factories. Note that production may not necessarily take place at the factory where the weapon was designed (e.g. *Msta*-B was designed by Titan-Barrikady in Volgograd, but almost all production took place at Motovilikha in Perm).

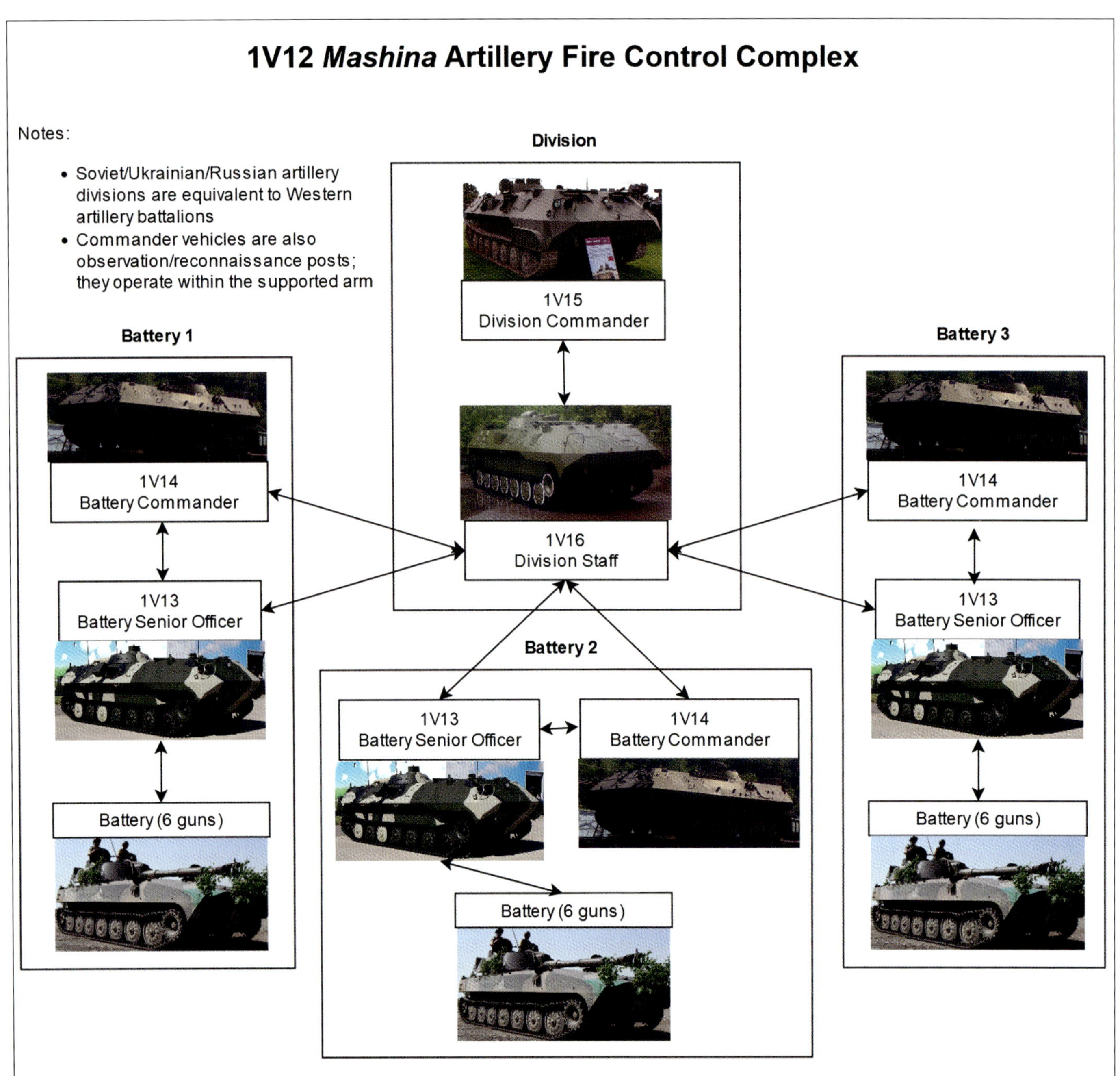

Mashina (1V12) fire control automation complex. These vehicles are still used by both Russia and Ukraine today, though not necessarily in the traditional ACRV/fire direction centre/command post roles, as UASs have largely taken over the reconnaissance role. *Mashina* primarily operated in support of Soviet tracked SPGs; the equivalent for towed artillery was *Mashina*-B (1V17), which has similar command vehicles based on BTR-60 APCs and trucks such as the ZIL-131 and GAZ-66. (Photo credits: Vitaly Kuzmin (1V13); 'Simon Q' (1V15); 'Smell U Later' (1V14 & 1V16))

Left: Russian 130mm M-46 operating in Kursk *oblast* during the Ukrainian invasion of Russia, August 2024. Long retired from Russian service, some M-46s have been 'resurrected' to help make up for losses. Ukraine also operates several M-46s donated by Finland, Macedonia, and Croatia. Right: M107 SPG in Vietnam, 1968. Despite problems with excessive barrel wear, the M107's outstanding 33km range left an impression on the Soviets via their allies who faced it. (MORF; USAHEC)

Technical Summary (*Giatsint*-B)

In order to achieve the range required, *Giatsint*-B uses a long L/50 monobloc barrel paired with a powerful charge: *Giatsint*'s 4Zh47 full charge weighs over double that of the D-20's (34.8kg vs. ~16kg). Thus, *Giatsint* uses a completely separate family of ammunition non-interchangeable with other Soviet 152mm pieces like the D-20 and *Msta*. It is capable of throwing the standard 46kg 3OF29 *Bekas* HE-Frag projectile at a muzzle velocity of 945m/s out to 28.5km. *Giatsint* is thus rated as a 'true' gun, not a hybrid 'gun-howitzer'. Longer ranges (up to 33km) are also possible using the 3OF30 *Baklan* RAP. A multi-slotted muzzle brake is fitted, which dissipates 53 percent of the ferocious recoil.

Ukrainian *Giatsint*-B fires at Russian forces on the Donetsk front, March 2023. Unusually, this *Giatsint*-B belongs to a motorised infantry brigade; they are usually found in artillery brigades. (ArmyInform)

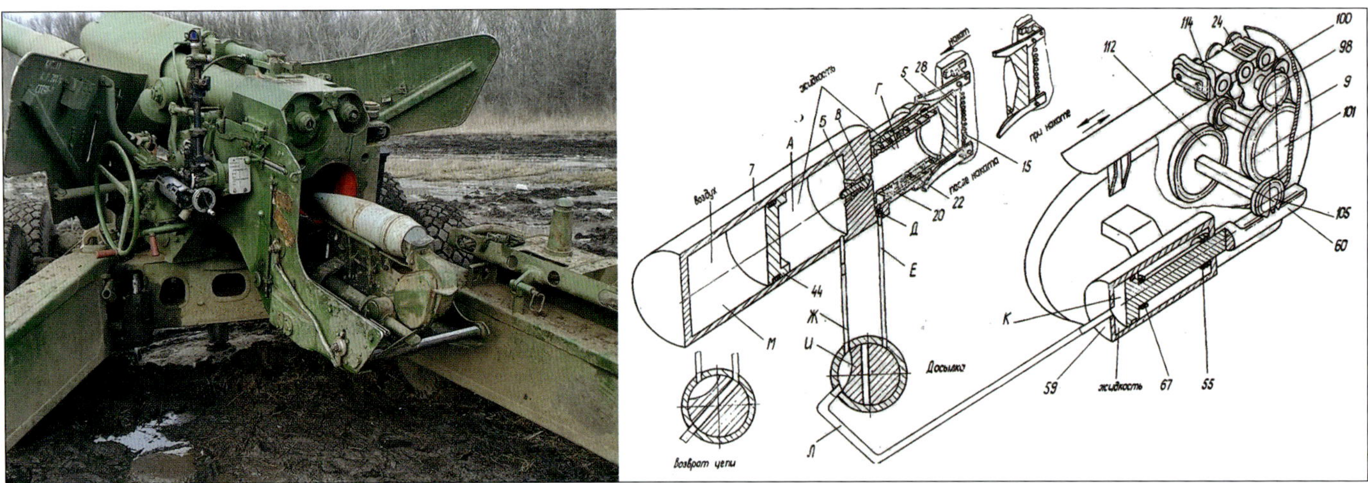

3OF29 *Bekas* HE shell placed in the *Giatsint*-B's rammer. The gunner's position can also be seen as well; the direct-fire sight is not fitted. The green tube above the recoil mechanism is the hydropneumatic accumulator, whose operation illustrated in this diagram from the manual on the right. (MOU; author's collection)

Giatsint-B features a chain rammer to assist with loading the heavy rounds. It is powered by a 'hydro-pneumatic accumulator', which stores the gun's recoil energy using compressed air. According to the author's NHU acquaintance, in his experience the rammer is quite prone to failure. It is thus more common to see *Giatsint*-Bs on both sides being manually loaded the old-fashioned way with a ramrod. In such cases, the rammer simply serves as a holder preventing the projectile or charge from slipping out of position. The gun has a horizontal-sliding block breech, and is rated for 5–6 rounds/minute. Indirect fire is conducted using the D-726-45/PG-1M sight while direct fire is done with the OP4M-90A telescopic sight. The gun can elevate up to 57° and has a traverse arc of +/-25°. The traverse has two speed settings; elevation has a fixed gear. The regular speed is for normal aiming, while the fast mode is for quickly getting the gun aimed in the rough bearing, though the author's NHU acquaintance states that the fast traverse was 'too taxing physically to be useful'.

Giatsint-B is much heavier than the D-20, weighing 9.8t. The distinctive carriage suspension consists of a pair of wheels with pneumatic tyres mounted on a balancer beam connected to a torsion bar on each side. It allows for high-speed towing, up to 60km/h on paved roads; there is no limber for towing, unlike with the M-46. Like the D-20, there is a pedestal baseplate with a hydraulic jack in

Deploying the *Giatsint*-B. The rammer automatically slides out of the breech's way when the breech is closed to allow the spent charge case to be ejected after firing. After firing, it will return to the loading line. (MOU)

the front of the carriage to provide stability when firing, with wheels raised off the ground. Because of its long-range, direct-fire anti-tank capability or rapid shifting of fire was not envisaged for the *Giatsint* family, and *Giatsint*-B thus lacks the trail rollers found on the D-20. They are also not issued with HEAT rounds. *Giatsint*-B has a crew of eight; emplace/displacement time is no more than 2–4 minutes in the manual, although the author's acquaintance says a trained crew can do this in half the time.

Technical Summary (*Giatsint*-S)

Giatsint-S's 152mm 2A37 is essentially identical to *Giatsint*-B's ordnance. Unlike the *Akatsiya*'s 2A33 howitzer, the 2A37 is placed in an open mounting on top of the *Giatsint*-S chassis' rear and has a limited traverse of +/-15° and up to 57° elevation. In order to fire the gun, the gunner must exit the armoured hull and use the controls on the gun's left. The position is protected by a small shield from the front, but is otherwise exposed. The sights are the same as those of the towed *Giatsint*-B. To help absorb the ferocious recoil, a rear support baseplate is provided, which is lowered before the gun is fired. The gun elevation and baseplate mechanisms are powered by a hydraulic drive derived from the *Tyulpan*, which also drives the magazines; traverse is manual. It is expected to take at most two minutes to emplace/displace a *Giatsint*-S.

Russian *Giatsint*-Ss of the Central Military District firing at Ukrainian targets, January 2023. *Giatsint*-S's long range exceeds that of the newer *Msta* family with unassisted projectiles. (MORF)

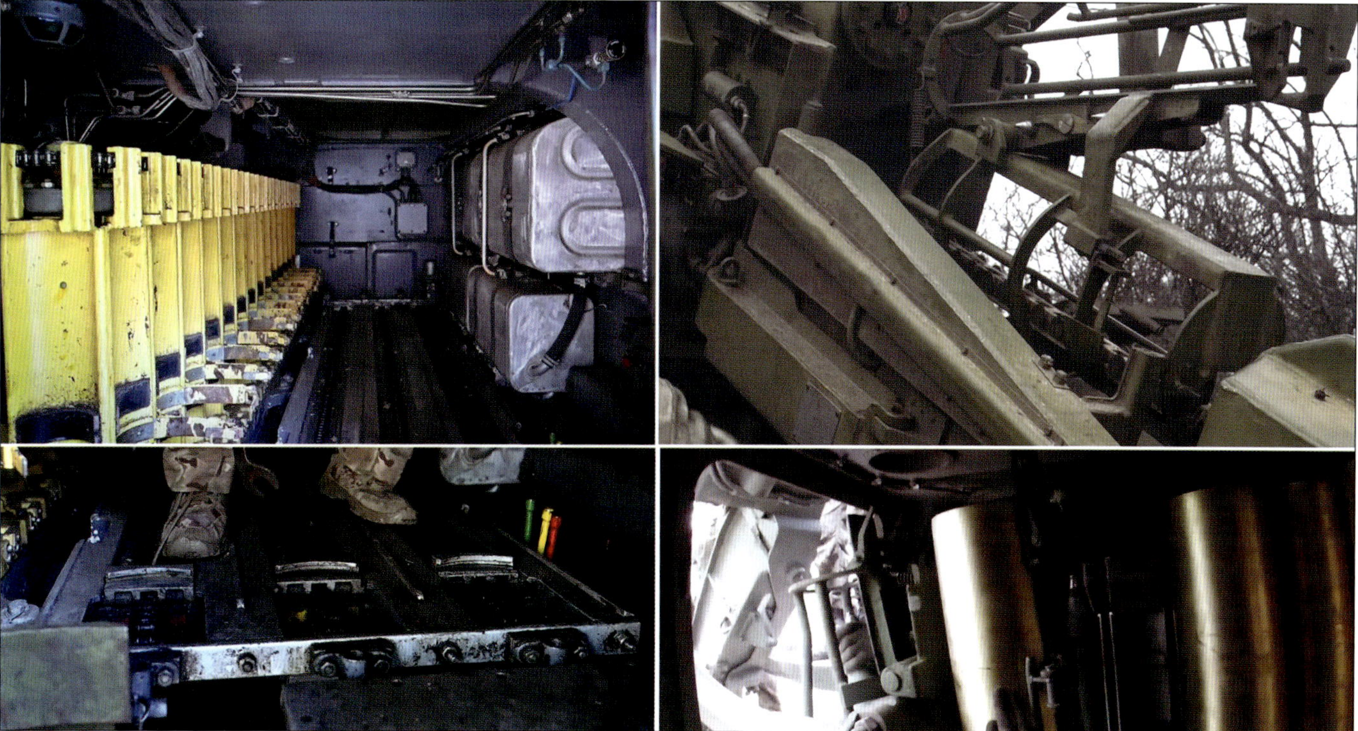

Left: ammunition stowage arrangement within a *Giatsint*-S. The last picture is from the point of view of the second loader, who is holding one of the large charge cases. Bottom: *Giatsint*-S's feeder and rammer; note the hole in the feeder cages for the chain rammer to pass through. The rammer is attached to the left of the gun, while the feeder is attached to the right side. The feeder can be lowered into the rear hatch, allowing the loaders to load the gun without exiting the vehicle. (MORF)

Russian *Giatsint*-Ss prepare to open fire on Ukrainian forces somewhere in Ukraine, January 2023. The hull and chassis are externally identical to that of the *Tyulpan*'s. (MORF)

A total of 30 rounds are carried within the vehicle: the projectiles are stored vertically in a conveyor belt-like rack located on the centreline of the hull, while the charges are also stored vertically to the right side of the shells on another conveyor rack on the hull floor. They are accessible via the rear hatch. *Giatsint*-S was designed with a semi-automatic loading system: a two-tray feeder mechanism attached to a lever arm on the gun's right brings the rounds up to be rammed into the gun, with two loaders transferring rounds from the conveyor magazines to the feeder under armour. However, this does not seem to be commonly done. An electrically-powered chain rammer is attached to the gun's left to ram the projectile and charge sequentially as they are brought in to the loading line by the feeder. The rate-of-fire is given as 5–6 rounds/minute.

The *Giatsint*-S is automotively identical to the *Akatsiya* and *Tyulpan*, thus the reader is asked to refer to the *Akatsiya* section for details on the V-59U engine and other automotive elements. *Giatsint*-S is slightly heavier than *Akatsiya* (28.2t), thus has a slightly lower power/weight ratio (18.4hp/t): this does not seem to affect its mobility noticeably. The hull is configured similarly to the *Tyulpan*, except it now has enough room inside to carry the entire crew of five. It has the same basic armour and even retains the commander's cupola with remote-controlled PKT machine gun. The rear compartment also contains an RPG-7 AT grenade launcher (five grenades) and a *Strela*-2 (9K32) MANPADS (two missiles) for self-defence. Communications equipment consists of the standard *Magnolia*-M radio and *Lebed* intercom.

Context

Second only to the much rarer *Pion* in range among Soviet-legacy guns available to Russia or Ukraine, *Giatsints* were and still are an important supplement to the D-20/*Akatsiya* and later *Msta*-B/S. In the 1980s, *Giatsints* enjoyed a substantial range advantage over their NATO equivalents, which mostly consisted of 155mm L/39 pieces such as the M109 SPG and French TRF1 towed gun. Their long range allowed them to be sited well behind the frontline, where there is less risk of both detection and counterbattery fire, while simultaneously enabling them to interdict shorter ranged enemy artillery. As such, the *Giatsint*-S's limited traverse and relative lack of protection compared to the *Akatsiya* and the large bulk of the *Giatsint*-B were much less of a concern. While the *Giatsints* use ammunition incompatible with those of other 152mm guns and also suffer from reduced barrel life (1,000–1,200 rounds) due to the 'hot' charges they use, their long range was considered worth these limitations.[11]

It appears that most, if not all, Russian *Giatsint*-B towed guns were in deep storage pre-2022, for the Warfare.ru table lists only 188 in five units, and they were not seen in VSRF use prior to the invasion. *Giatsint*-S was slightly more common at 221 in six units, but it has been consistently seen in official MORF media releases pre-2022, primarily based in the Eastern Military District. While there have been proposed Russian upgrade packages for both *Giatsints* that incorporate things such as modern extended-range ammunition, automated gun-laying, and improved navigation systems, these do not appear to have been pursued so far. Development efforts have been focused on the *Msta* family and the new *Koalitsiya*-SV, and it was at one point expected that they would completely replace the *Giatsints*. However, the heavy losses the VSRF has experienced since the 2022 invasion mean that no Russian artillery piece can be spared, thus both types are being used by the VSRF in Ukraine at the time of writing. Very recently, the Russians have also combined the *Giatsint*-B's ordnance with the *Malva* wheeled SPG's chassis to create the *Giatsint*-K (see '*Koalitsiya* & *Malva*' box). The Luhansk and Donetsk militants also operated *Giatsint*-Bs during the Donbas War.[12]

Giatsint-S is rarely seen in Ukrainian service, as Ukraine inherited relatively few of these SPGs post-1991 (24).[13] This is further compounded by the fact that both the chassis and gun are manufactured only in Russia, which makes spare parts harder to come by. The few in active service were used quite intensively during the Donbas War, and mostly worn out by 2022. Several Russian *Giatsint*-Ss were captured during the fall 2022 Kharkiv counteroffensive and are actively used, but they remain very rare.[14] *Giatsint*-B is significantly more common in Ukrainian service (claimed to be 270 inherited post-1991) and remains an important part of the ZSU's artillery park.[15] Interestingly, the Ukrainians also unveiled a new towed howitzer in September 2024 that combined the *Giatsint*-B's carriage with a domestic 155mm L/52 from the *Bohdana* SPG.[16] It is not yet known if all *Giatsints* will be converted to this ordnance in the future.

Today, the range advantage *Giatsints* have historically enjoyed has largely disappeared with the advent of next-generation NATO 155mm L/52 artillery, such as those found on the CAESAR and PzH 2000. They are capable of firing out to 30km with standard projectiles and in excess of 50km with extended-range munitions, far in excess of what *Giatsints* are capable of with their own RAP. Some of these systems are currently being used by the Ukrainians, as will be detailed in a later chapter. However, their numbers are not currently very large (as is the stock of extended-range munitions), and the bulk of the artillery used by both sides remains Soviet-legacy pieces. More challenging is the proliferation of reconnaissance and combat UASs: the large sizes of the *Giatsint*s mean that good camouflage is essential to avoid detection and destruction. Still, they can be placed further from the frontline than shorter ranged pieces like the D-20 or older M109 models, which is in itself a form of protection, and their range advantage over most other common Soviet-legacy pieces should keep them relevant to this war as long as they can be logistically supported.

Russian *Giatsint*-B of the 14th 'Kalmius' Guards Artillery Brigade, July 2022. The brigade was formerly part of the Donetsk People's Militia, but was absorbed into the VSRF after the 2022 invasion. The long barrel appears to have been painted to resemble a tree trunk as camouflage. (MORF)

Ukrainian *Giatsint*-S of 26 Art. with support baseplate deployed, pre-2022 invasion. The plaque says 'PTN PNKh', an abbreviation of the slogan '*Putin poshyol nakhuy*' ('Putin, go fuck yourself'). (Sprotyv.info)

6
PION: BRINGING DOWN THE HAMMER

Development History

As noted in the *Giatsint* section, in the late 1960s, the Soviets had begun developing new long-range guns in response to the American M107. The US had also deployed the 8-inch Self-Propelled Heavy Howitzer M110, which had a shorter ranged 8-inch (203mm) M2A2 L/25 howitzer but could fire a heavier 90.7kg M106 HE-Frag projectile at 594m/s out to 16.8km.[1] Notably, it could fire a nuclear shell (M422 (W33)), which the M107 lacked. Both systems shared the same highly mobile tracked chassis.[2] At that time, the Soviets' only answer available in significant numbers was the 203mm B-4M towed howitzer, whose L/25 ordnance dated back to 1931. It could fire a 100kg shell out to 18km, but as an 18.7t towed piece it had neither the mobility of the M110 or range of the M107.[3]

Pion of the 43rd 'Hetman Taras Triasylo' Artillery Brigade preparing to fire, July 2022. The *Pion* is the heaviest and longest ranged Soviet-legacy artillery gun to be used in the war. (43 Art., Facebook)

Left: 203mm B-4 operating near Moscow, February 1942. Modernised with a wheeled carriage in 1955, it would remain the primary Soviet heavy artillery piece until the 1970s. Right: Dutch M110 SPG with the original M2A2 howitzer. The later M110A2 would receive the M201A1 L/37 howitzer, which could achieve 25km range with unassisted projectiles. (RIAN; Dutch MoD)

The Soviets did already have the 180mm S-23, a 21.5t L/48 towed gun whose range exceeded 30km with the 88kg F-572 HE shell fired at 860m/s. However, only eight guns were built by 1955 before the S-23 fell victim to Khrushchev, and they were relegated to parade duty by 1967.[4] It was also still a towed gun, and took 30 minutes to emplace/displace.[5] That same year, LKZ's KB-3 design bureau under Nikolai Popov, on its own initiative, proposed a 203mm '*SAU osoboy moshchnosti*' ('special power SPG') based on the T-64A (GBTU: 434) MBT chassis. Unfortunately, the design had many defects and would not get very far, especially after Defence Minister Andrei Grechko reportedly said '*Chto eto za gumno*?' ('What kind of trash is this?') upon examining the full-scale wooden model.[6] Still, the concept warranted further study, and work continued with official backing.

The requirements issued at this time were quite vague, only specifying a range of at least 25km but not the gun or chassis. The project, codenamed *Pion* ('Peony'), investigated various armaments, but eventually narrowed down to two: 180mm S-23 (*Pion*-1) and a new 203mm gun (*Pion*-2).[7] [8] By early 1969, the latter option was chosen, and development of the *Pion* (GRAU: 2S7, GBTU: 216) was formally authorised in 1970, with KB-3 tasked as overall project lead and *Barrikady*'s OKB-2 design bureau under Georgiy Sergeev the 203mm gun.[9] Chassis choice and configuration was also subject to fierce debate: options discussed included the T-64A, the MT-T *Yeney* tractor, and then one (GBTU: 216 *sp.* 1) derived from LKZ's T-10M heavy tank with the gun frontally mounted in an armoured casemate.[10] Finally, they settled on a new chassis (GBTU: 216 sp. 2) with the gun in a rear open mounting with elements derived from the T-80 and T-72 MBTs, then also under development.[11] [12]

The tactical-technical requirements for the *Pion* were thus finalised by 1973 and two prototypes completed that year; after testing and modifications, it was accepted into service in 1975, although the nuclear munitions designed specifically for it did not become available until 1977.[13] In 1983, the improved *Malka* (GRAU: 2S7M; GBTU: 216M) was accepted into service, though it did not enter series production until 1986.[14] This variant has mostly internal changes to the engine, fire control, ammunition stowage, and crew accommodation: the author is not currently aware of any 'easy' or consistent identification markers between *Pion* and *Malka*. For the rest of this section, unless otherwise specified, the author shall generically refer to both as '*Pion*'. *Pions* were built in relatively small numbers, estimated at over 500 before production ended in 1990. The unit cost was ₽521,527 in 1990.[15]

Technical Summary

The *Pion*'s 203mm 2A44 gun has an L/55 barrel. Combined with the 44kg full propellant charge, it can hurl the 110kg 3OF43 *Albatros* HE-Frag shell at 960m/s out to over 37km. With the 3OF44 *Burevestnik*-2 RAP this can be extended to 47.5km. This comes at the cost of a low barrel life of only 400–500 rounds before replacement is required.[16] Unusually (for a Soviet land artillery gun) the *Pion* does not use cased charges: instead, it has bagged charges with an inserted electric primer. Thus, the 2A44 uses a mechanised interrupted screw breech. The 2A44 is mounted externally on the hull and can be elevated up to 60° and traversed +/-15° by the gunner, who must exit the vehicle and operate the gun and its rammer from a platform on the gun's left. The rammer is mounted on a lever arm attached the gun's right and allows loading at any elevation angle. The original *Pion* has a maximum rate-of-fire of 1.5–2 rounds/minute, while the modernised *Malka* has an improved rammer and automatically-opening breech, increasing the rate-of-fire to 2.5 rounds/minute.[17] [18] Greater automation of the loading process was also introduced: instead of having a button or switch for each step of the loading process, the *Malka*'s rammer control panel simplified this down to two buttons (one for projectile loading, the other for the charge).[19]

The original *Pion* carries only four rounds within the vehicle; *Malka* doubles this to eight. These rounds cannot be loaded from within the vehicle and must be brought outside: *Pions* operate exclusively in 'shooting from the ground' mode, with most ammunition supplied externally from a separate transport vehicle (a typical load is 40 rounds).[20] Aiming instruments include the usual D-726-45/PG-1M sight for indirect fire, as well as the OP4M-99A telescopic sight for direct fire.[21] In addition to the standard *Magnolia*-M radio and *Lebed* crew intercom found on *Pions*, *Malkas* are also equipped with the 1V522 targeting data receiver. It serves the same function as the 1V159 on *Akatsiyas* upgraded to the 2S3M1 standard and is a part of the *Mekhanizator* set linking *Malkas* to the 1V13M platoon command vehicles' 1V158 transceiver.[22] As with the 2S3M1, it significantly improved the reaction times and accuracy of networked *Malkas*.

The *Pion*'s chassis utilises many of the T-80's suspension components, including the rubber-rimmed forged aluminium roadwheels (*Pion* has seven, as opposed to six on the T-80), double-pin 'live' tracks with rubber bushings and inner rubber pads, telescoping hydraulic shock absorbers on the first and last two road wheels, and torsion bar suspension. To withstand the massive recoil (135 tf), the *Pion* is equipped with a hydraulic rear spade and the rear idler wheels are also lowered hydraulically to the ground when

180mm S-23 at the Qala'at Salah ad-Din, Cairo, Egypt. S-23 production was reactivated after 1973 specifically for export to Egypt and Syria, as it was the only Soviet artillery piece at the time that could even hope to counterbattery Israeli M107s. (Zienauto)

The massive fireball created by a *Pion* firing; a muzzle brake was considered, but during testing the resulting muzzle blast overpressure seriously damaged the driver's cabin and it was abandoned. (43 Art.)

Top: the gunner's station on a *Pion*. Behind him is a platform from which the rammer is operated, as seen in the bottom picture illustrating the rammer. (43 Art.; MOU)

A trolley is used to cart the heavy shells to the *Pion* where the tray can be levered onto the rammer. It is also possible to detach the tray and carry the shell on the frame like a stretcher. The chain rammer is then brought in line with the gun to load the shell, while the charges (No. 3 charge seen here) are light enough to be man-handled. (MORF)

the spade is deployed to provide extra stability.[23] It is, however, possible to fire the weapon safely without lowering the spade and wheels if only the minimum charge is used.[24] The nominal time to emplace/displace the *Pion* is 10 minutes, while the *Malka* improved this to 5–6 and 3–5 minutes, respectively.[25]

Unlike the T-80, V-12 diesel engines from the T-72 MBT family are used instead of a gas turbine. The original 45t *Pion* uses the 780hp V-46-1, while the heavier 46.5t modernised *Malka* has the 840hp V-84B, providing a power/weight ratio of 17–18hp/t.[26] The engine is mounted behind the front control compartment, providing space for the 2A44 gun and helping to balance its weight. The transmission is of the BKP (*bortovoy korobki peredach* – lit. 'side/attached gearbox') type common to all Soviet MBTs since the T-64, with seven forward and one reverse gear providing a top road speed of 50km/h. *Pions* and *Malkas* also have a 24hp 9R4-6U2 APU to power the electrical and hydraulic systems when the engine is turned off.

It is easy to see the lineage of the *Pion's* running gear (top) from that of the T-80 MBT (bottom), though the *Pion*'s chassis is longer and has an extra road wheel and return roller. (MORF; Kirill Koksharov)

The *Pion*'s hull (GBTU: 216-50-sb2) is made out of two layers of armour plate: outer 13mm and inner 8mm. These protect the crew of seven (six for the *Malka*) against small arms fire and shell splinters. The hull also provides NBC protection for the entire crew, who can all be seated internally but must exit the vehicle to operate the SPG.[27] *Pions* also carry a 12.7mm *Utyos* heavy AAMG and *Strela*-2 or *Igla* (9K38) MANPADS for self-defence, but the author has so far not seen any photos of either being used.[28]

Context

If the Soviets regarded their artillery as 'gods' of war, then the *Pion* certainly has good claim to being the 'Zeus' of the late Cold War Soviet artillery pantheon. Its combination of exceptionally long range and a hard-hitting shell is unmatched among Soviet-legacy artillery pieces currently in service. A single projectile from the *Pion* is claimed to be sufficient to destroy a command post in a two-story building or a concrete-hardened command post.[29] It currently has no real equivalent in Western militaries, who have mostly retired artillery pieces larger than 155mm. It was not until the introduction of 155mm L/52 pieces after the Cold War that Western artillery was able to match or exceed its long range.

In Soviet times, the *Pion* was used exclusively by the ARVGK's high-power artillery brigades. As with the *Tyulpan*, these would prosecute high-value or hardened targets beyond the capabilities of standard divisional 122/152mm guns. According to Shirokorad, 347 were in service in 1990, with 307 of these located west of the Urals.[30] After 1991, Russia is believed to have inherited the majority of the USSR's *Pions*. In 2008, there were at least 37 *Pions* known to be in active Russian service, of which 12 were in 45 High-Power Art. along with the *Tyulpans*. They were retired from active service in 2009 when the brigade was disbanded, but returned to service in 2017 when the brigade was reestablished. It was also planned to integrate these into the YeSU TZ BMS, but it remains an open question to what level this was achieved.[31]

Ukraine has also inherited a significant number of *Pions*: 99 according to Zhirokhov, with six of these being sold to Georgia prior to the 2008 Russian invasion, plus several more to Azerbaijan. The rest were placed into storage following Ukraine's independence and 1992 ratification of the CFE: in fact, they were ordered to be scrapped at one point, but fortunately for the Ukrainians the order was not carried out. Following the 2014 Russian invasion, several were reactivated and formed into the 5th artillery division of 26 Art. in November 2014 (a Soviet-style artillery brigade normally has four artillery divisions, which are equivalent to artillery battalions in most Western armies). This division was later expanded into its own independent brigade, the 43rd 'Hetman Taras Triasylo' Artillery Brigade.[32] At the time of writing, it remains the only Ukrainian unit to operate the *Pion*, though since 2022 it also operates the German PzH 2000 alongside them.

Ukraine began using its *Pions* in combat during the latter stages of the Donbas War until the Minsk II accords came into effect in February 2015. They also played an important role in blunting and ultimately defeating the initial Russian attempt to subjugate Ukraine in 2022. In particular, three of 43 Art.'s batteries (3 x 4 guns) were committed during the defence of Kyiv, inflicting significant damage on Russian forces during the battles for Hostomel, Bucha, and Brovary. They continue to serve in the ZSU, although ammunition and spare barrel availability remain key issues. Less is known about their Russian counterparts' activities, but it does not appear that the Russian *Pions* were committed to battle until after the failure of the initial February invasion: 43 Art.'s commanding officer, Brigadier General Oleg Shevchuk noted that none were encountered during the battle for Kyiv.[33]

As powerful as the *Pion* is, there are some notable limitations to the platform's capabilities. The first and arguably most serious one is the lack of guided shells: for unclear reasons, the Soviets, Russians, and Ukrainians have never fielded any, unlike the other calibres. Secondly, at the time of writing, both Ukrainian and Russian forces appear to be running short of 203mm ammunition. Ironically, both

Russian *Pion* of the Southern Group (Donetsk front) being fired from a prepared position using a lanyard, February 2024. The video description claims this to be a *Malka*, but it does not have an automatically-opening breech, making it an older *Pion*. (MORF)

have also turned to an unlikely source for a temporary remedy: the US. Photographic evidence has been published of the American 8-inch M106 HE-Frag projectile being used by both sides.[34] [35] The Ukrainians received these either directly from the US, which still maintains a stockpile despite no longer fielding 8-inch weapons, but the Russian source is less clear: likely Iran, which received M110s from the US before the 1979 revolution. However, Andriy Kobzar, a former gunner in 43 Art., noted in an interview that M106 shells have thinner walls and are must be fired at reduced charge to avoid the shell bursting in the barrel, which reduces the range the *Pion* can achieve.[36] Lastly, the *Pion* is a very large system (over 10m long, 3m wide), making it quite difficult to conceal from aerial surveillance. However, this is partly negated by the very long range, which allows it to be deployed in less vulnerable rear locations beyond the reach of most counterbattery artillery fire, especially the Soviet-legacy pieces that predominate in the VSRF.

The *Pion* provides a unique long-range heavyweight punch for both Ukrainian and Russian militaries. However, it is very much a limited resource for both sides, as the production line for both guns and ammunition has long been closed, and also due to the low barrel life. It is believed by some, such as Professor Andriy Kharuk, that Russia has obtained *Juche'po* SPGs from the DPRK to replace its dwindling numbers of *Pions* (see *Juche'po* box).[37] Given the relatively small numbers in service, it is questionable whether either side will invest in rebuilding the production lines from scratch to properly sustain these weapons over the long term. Nevertheless, the *Pion*'s unmatched brute power will always find a use for as long as it is serviceable.

'*Skif*' ('Scythian') of 43 Art., winter 2023. The long-term future of the *Pion* is uncertain, but for now it remains a valuable, hard-hitting long-range weapon for both sides. (43 Art.)

JUCHE'PO: THE MYSTERIOUS BEAST FROM THE EAST

Due to the closed nature of the so-called 'hermit kingdom', exact information about DPRK weapon system specifications and development history is very scarce and difficult to verify. This applies to the mysterious *Juche'po*, a long-range 170mm SPG that the DPRK has begun supplying to Russia along with Korean People's Army (KPA) soldiers to join the Russo-Ukrainian War. The KPA places great importance on massed artillery fires, with large ammunition stockpiles and artillery parks, as well as domestic manufacturing capacity for both; 'Supreme Leader' and 'Brilliant Comrade' Kim Jong-Un himself has stated: 'Modern warfare is an artillery battle', and regularly conducts inspections of KPA artillery troops.[38] Thus, the DPRK is one of the few countries with the capability and willingness to supply Russia with artillery at scale, having begun sending artillery ammunition in September 2023.[39] Despite the reportedly questionable quality of North Korean ammunition, its importance to the Russian war effort cannot be overstated. The appearance of the *Juche'po* in Russia marks a natural and unsurprising escalation of the DPRK's assistance.

Exactly when the *Juche'po* began development and entered service are not publicly unknown, but the first KPA 170mm SPG was detected by US intelligence in 1978 in the city of Koksan; it was thus assigned the name 'M1978 Koksan' by the US, which remains the name usually used in Western publications.[40] This was followed by a redesigned version using the same gun, first spotted in 1989 (hence 'M1989 Koksan').[41] The name '*Juche'po*' (lit. '*Juche* gun', '*Juche*' being the DPRK's autarkic state ideology) itself is uncertain as an official KPA designation, for it is only based on placards mounted on the SPGs during parades.[42] The original *Juche'po* was a rather simple vehicle, being essentially a somewhat modified Chinese Type 59 (T-54 copy) MBT with the massive 170mm gun in a limited-traverse mounting on sliding rails, rear hydraulic spades, and a gun barrel travel lock. The so-called 1989 version of the *Juche'po* appears to have been inspired by the Soviet *Pion* SPG's configuration: it utilises a longer redesigned chassis, with the engine and transmission now placed behind a crew cabin similar in design to the *Pion*'s, but seems to reuse suspension components from the original.

The 170mm gun is somewhat of a mystery itself. It has been variously speculated that the gun may be based on captured Second World War German 17cm K 18 guns (no other nation has previously developed artillery of this calibre) provided by the Soviets, Japanese 15cm Type 96 coastal defence guns left in the DPRK after the Second World War, or Soviet 180mm naval and land guns, but there is no hard evidence for any of these.[43] Jiarui Zhang and Danyi Fu have noted the close similarity of the gun's recoil mechanism to the K 18's.[44] Chinese online circles have also speculated that the gun was made from two 180mm barrels spliced together, with a liner reducing the diameter to 170mm in order to smooth the splicing out.[45] What is certain is that it has a

'89 *Juche'po* seen during a DPRK parade in 2012. Much remains to be learned about the system, which is considerably different to the older version used by Iran. (Top81.cn)

very long barrel; though no exact figures are publicly available, measurements from images give an estimated length of about 70 calibres, and this is also the figure given by Zhang & Fu. It has an interrupted screw breech and either a multi-slotted or double-baffle muzzle brake. Unlike the *Pion*, there does not appear to be any semi-automatic loader or rammer, thus loading would be done entirely manually. The rate-of-fire is therefore usually estimated at a rather glacial 1–2 rounds every five minutes. However, this remains to be confirmed.

The gun is usually credited with a range of 43km with unassisted HE shells and 54–66km using RAPs;[46] it is generally thought that the DPRK originally designed it as deterrent against the Republic of Korea (ROK) by being able to shell Seoul, the ROK capital city, from behind the DPRK/ROK demilitarised zone.[47] However, when compared to the 175mm M107 (32.8km) or 203mm *Pion* SPGs (37km, 47.5km assisted), it is difficult to see how this range can be achieved without sacrificing barrel life (more propellant = more barrel pressure = more barrel wear), explosive filler weight (to achieve greater range with rocket assist, more space must be sacrificed in the shell for rocket fuel instead of explosive filler), accuracy (lighter shells are more affected by wind and other meteorological factors over long ranges), or all three. All of these would significantly impact the military utility of the weapon.

It is impossible to say for certain what trade-offs the DPRK engineers made in order to achieve the remarkably long ranges credited to the *Juche'po* until greater information is available on the ammunition it uses.[48] The only information on the ammunition comes from Abdul Hamid Tarakh on the Iranian website Jangaavaran, who states that it weighs about 80kg and contains 10–12kg explosive.[49] Given data for the M107 (67kg M437 HE with 13.6kg filler; 23kg propellant charge), this most likely refers to the standard HE shell weight combined with the propellant charge; thus, the 170mm HE shell has a similar filler content to the standard US 155mm HE shell (M795; 10.8kg filler). The author's Fermi estimate is that the shell weighs ~55kg if one assumes the filler/shell weight percentage at about 20 percent. Fredenburg estimates the weight at ~61kg, but this is too heavy for the remaining propellant to give it the 43km range, if Tarakh is correct. As far as is publicly known, there is no PGM available for the *Juche'po*.

The '78 *Juche'po* first saw combat during the Iran-Iraq War, with the DPRK shipping at least 20 to Iran to be used during the battles for the Faw Peninsula and Basra. Some were captured by Iraqi forces, who then allowed US intelligence to evaluate it.[50] Tarakh notes that the weapon had poor accuracy and a low rate-of-fire, and it seems to have mostly been used as a harassment weapon against Kuwaiti oilfields and the Iraqi city of Basra. However, the '89 *Juche'po* has never previously been exported nor has it seen combat; thus, it remains an unknown quantity, despite being a regular guest in DPRK parades. In November 2024, a photo of two *Juche'pos* on a train surfaced, subsequently geolocated to Krasnoyarsk, Russia.[51] It is claimed that Russia has received as many as 62 *Juche'pos* and that they will most likely be sent to Kursk *oblast*, where KPA forces are known to have been sent as well.[52] At the time of writing, no footage of the system in combat has surfaced, nor is it known whether the system is being used with North Korean or Russian crews. It remains to be seen whether the '89 *Juche'po* will perform better than the '78 did in Iran.

7
NONA: THE UNIVERSAL WEAPON

Development History

The Soviets, pioneers in the development of airborne forces, have long wrestled with problem of providing the VDV with sufficient firepower that could be dropped along with them during a landing operation. In the 1950s and 1960s, the primary source of artillery pieces used by the VDV were mortars, 122mm D-30 howitzers, 'self-moving' guns with motors such as the 57mm SD-57 AT gun and 85mm SD-44 field gun, and SPGs such as the ASU-57 and SU-85.[1] The latter were primarily designed for direct fire, like other contemporary Soviet SPGs, as were the motorised towed guns, which left only the mortars or D-30 as the primary means of indirect fire support.

In 1969, the BMD-1 (*boevaya mashina desanta* – 'landing combat vehicle'; GBTU: 915) airborne IFV was introduced into service. This vehicle was a quantum leap in capability for the VDV, combining the high firepower of its 73mm *Grom* (2A28) gun and *Malyutka* (9M14) ATGMs with excellent mobility thanks to its amphibious capabilities, hydropneumatic suspension, and high power/weight ratio. The BMD-1 could be dropped with its crew and a paratrooper squad inside the vehicle, ready for combat almost from the moment the vehicle touched the ground. However, it also meant that the towed D-30s or mortars no longer had the mobility to keep up with the BMD-1s, since they had to be dropped separately from their crews. Furthermore, they lacked NBC protection, an important consideration given the new vision for the VDV under General Vasiliy Margelov as a rapid reaction force that could quickly occupy territory following a nuclear strike.[2]

Attempts were made to create an airborne SP platform using the D-30 howitzer; while the *Gvozdika* was successfully tested in airborne drops, it was too heavy to be dropped from an Antonov An-12 twin-engine transport aircraft. The *Fialka* ('Violet'; GRAU: 2S2; GBTU: 924) project was authorised in 1967: a casemate SPG using a modified D-30 with limited traverse based on the BMD-1 chassis. However, the prototypes proved unable to withstand the D-30's recoil during testing, and the *Fialka* was cancelled in 1968. In 1969, another project known as *Landish* ('Lily of the Valley'; GRAU: 2S8) based on the *Fialka*, but armed with a 120mm smoothbore mortar, was started. It proved unable meet the requirements for gun traverse angles or the ability to mount a 12.7mm *Utyos* machine gun and, furthermore, it was felt that 120mm smoothbore mortars had exhausted their development potential.[3]

At around the same time, the Soviets became interested in the new French *mortier de* 120 mm *rayé tracté modèle* F1 ('120 mm towed rifled mortar model F1'; MO 120 RTF1 or simply RTF1 for short), also known by the manufacturer (Thomson-Brandt) designation MO-120-RT-61. As the name might suggest, the RTF1 had a *rifled* barrel, as opposed to conventional mortars with smoothbore barrels. Its primary projectile, the OE FMP 120 PRY F1, was more akin to conventional artillery shells, stabilised by the spin imparted by the shell and RTF1's barrel rifling instead of fins found

Russian VDV *Nona*-S during joint exercises with Belarusian special forces, Pskov, October 2017. The diminutive size of the *Nona*-S can be seen in comparison with the driver. (MORF)

Top: 57mm SD-57 'self-moving' AT gun at the Memorial Mound of Glory in Pereiaslav-Khmelnytskyi, Ukraine; essentially a towed gun with a motorcycle engine attached for limited mobility on the battlefield. Long distance movements were intended to be carried out using prime movers like a regular towed piece. Bottom: the SU-85 was primarily designed for direct fire support of the VDV's paratroopers. While it is commonly known as the 'ASU-85', it is only ever referred to as 'SU-85' in its manuals. (Pavlo1; Vitaliy Kuzmin)

BMD-1P used for driver training at the Odesa Military Academy, March 2017. Designed to provide the same level of mobility and firepower as the BMP-1 IFV at just over half the weight. (Serhii Danilenko, MOU)

on conventional smoothbore mortar bombs.[4] This approach allows for more explosive filler and better fragmentation due to the more optimal projectile shape, as well as improved accuracy. It could reach 8km, or up to 13km with the rocket-assisted OE PAD FMP 120 PRY F2, thus giving the RTF1 capabilities comparable to a 105mm howitzer while weighing only 500–600kg.[5] Furthermore, the rifled barrel could still fire finned mortar bombs if needed.[6] The Soviets were able to acquire some of the RTF1's shells for testing through means (publicly) unknown and were impressed enough to consider making their own rifled mortar.[7]

Avenir Novozhilov, based at the Central Research Institute for Precision Engineering (*Tsentralniy nauchno-issledovatelskiy institute tochnogo mashinostryeoeniya,* TsNIITochmash) in Klimovsk (today part of Podolsk, Russia), proposed using a 120mm weapon based on the RTF1 for the new VDV SPG, codenamed *Nona*. 'Nona' is a common Russian girl's name; it is sometimes claimed that '*Nona*' is an acronym for '*Noveyshee orudie nazemnoy artillerii*' ('Newest ground artillery ordnance') or similar, but according to Veniamin Schastlivtsev, head of the artillery department at TsNIITochmash, the name was simply selected from a list of options presented by the GRAU to General Margelov, who reportedly said '*Nu chto zhe, navernoe, eto budet khoroshchaya devka*' ('Well, she'll probably be a good girl').[8]

In 1974, a proof-of-concept, *Nona*-D, mating the *Fialka*'s casemate superstructure with the extended chassis of the BTR-D (GBTU: 925) airborne APC and the 120mm rifled mortar was completed. Following successful tests, development of the *Nona*-S (GRAU: 2S9) airborne SPG was authorised in 1976. Initially, TsNIITochmash was to collaborate with OKB-9 to develop the 120mm 2A51 ordnance, but the latter refused further work after a leadership change. Thus, the Motovilikha factory and OKB-172 under Kalachnikov were brought in to help. The first prototype was completed in 1977. At the conclusion of these tests, the *Nona*-S was formally adopted for service in 1981.[9] In 1988, the *Sviristelka* ('Waxwing'; GRAU: 2S9-1) variant was produced specifically for the Soviet Marines.[10] By the time production ended in 1989, 1,432 *Nona-S*/*Sviristelkas* had been built.[11] Subsequently, in 2002 Russian *Nona*-Ss were upgraded to enable the use of the *Kitolov*-2 laser-guided PGM, while in 2008 the latest *Nona*-SM (GRAU: 2S9-1M) modernisation was adopted, with vehicles upgraded to this standard as they underwent overhaul.[12]

The Soviet Ground Forces (*Sukhoputnye voyska*, SV) also became interested in the new 'universal' weapon for use in a battalion-level SPG. In 1977, the *Nona*-SV project was initiated in two variants, one (GRAU: 2S17) based on the *Gvozdika*'s chassis, the other (GRAU: 2S17-2) based on the BRM-1K (GBTU: 676) artillery reconnaissance vehicle derived from the BMP-2 IFV. In the event, only a single prototype of the former was built in Soviet times, for it was decided that a wheeled chassis would be less complicated to maintain, faster on roads, and more importantly, cheaper since it had to be distributed widely at the battalion level. TsNII *Burevestnik* had proposed such a design as early as 1981, based on the BTR-70 8x8 APC, but in 1984 the new BTR-80 8x8 APC was chosen instead by the Soviet government under the name '*Nona*-SVK' ('K' for '*kolesnaya*'— 'wheeled'; GRAU: 2S23), to be developed once again by Motovilikha. The process of modifying the *Nona*-S's turret for use with the BTR-80 chassis was non-trivial and the new *Nona*-SVK was only adopted for service in 1991.[13] The USSR's collapse later that year effectively killed any hope for the system being put into mass

MO 120 RTF1 with the Kastuś Kalinoŭski Rgt., a Belarusian volunteer unit fighting for Ukraine, May 2023. The shell is an American-made M1101: the US Marine Corps used the RTF1 as the M327 120mm Expeditionary Fire Support System from 2009 to 2017. The rifling bands can be clearly seen, with the writing '*Po khoroshim russkim*' ('To the good Russians'). The coloured rings contain additional charges (colour denoting the amount), added according to the range and trajectory needed. (Kalinoŭski Rgt.)

Left: Ukraine does not produce the BMD/BTR-D family and has encountered problems maintaining its *Nona*-S fleet, particularly the complex hydropneumatic suspension. Some of their turrets have been removed and mounted on the BMP/BRM chassis, effectively resurrecting the *Nona*-SV project, seen here in March 2023. Right: *Nona*-SVK of the 55th Guards Motor-Rifle Brigade, Tuvan Republic, Russia, September 2020. Note that the turret is different to the *Nona*-S's. (25 Airborne; MORF)

service, though some motor-rifle units received it, including the 55th Independent Guards Mountain Motor-Rifle Brigade.[14] *Nona*-SVKs are also used in limited numbers by Russian Marine brigades.[15]

In addition to the SPGs, towed versions of the *Nona*'s ordnance have also been developed. The first of these was the *Nona*-K (GRAU: 2B16). Originally it was '*Nona*-B' in accordance with Soviet convention, but this was changed to '*Nona*-K' for unclear reasons.[16] It was apparently developed in response to combat experience from the Soviet-Afghan War, which highlighted the need for a light towed gun with comparable firepower to 122/152mm weapons.[17] *Nona*-K entered service in 1986, primarily with Soviet VDV and Marine units, but it was not produced in large numbers: according to the Motovilikha museum, only 188.[18] In the early 2000s, a towed breech-loading mortar based on the *Nona*'s ballistics was also developed, known as *Nona*-M1 (GRAU: 2B-23); with this, the *Nona* family comes full circle back to its origins in the RTF1. It entered Russian service in 2007 in limited numbers.[19]

Due to length limitations, the following technical summary will focus only on the *Nona*-S/SM and *Sviristelka* tracked SPGs (generically *Nona*-S), for they were by far the most common members of the *Nona* family in service at the start of the Russo-Ukrainian War. Although the various members of the *Nona* family use different platforms, their ordnances are ballistically identical and share ammunition, thus for all practical purposes they mostly provide similar indirect fire capabilities.

Technical Summary

The *Nona*-S's 120mm 2A51 is an L/24 breech-loaded rifled ordnance capable of firing a wide range of projectiles, from conventional finned mortar bombs to pre-rifled shells. Its standard projectile is the 19.8kg 3OF49 pre-rifled shell, which can be fired at a muzzle velocity of 367m/s out to a maximum range of 8.8km. This can be extended out to 12.8km using the 3OF50 pre-rifled RAP. The 2A51 has a somewhat unconventional semi-automatic breech mechanism with two breech blocks. The first is a round block with de Bange-type obturator ring attached to a moving cylinder. It not only seals the breech during firing but also functions as a rammer, powered by compressed air. This block has no locking mechanism, thus it is locked in place by a second vertical-sliding breech block. The maximum rate-of-fire given in the manual is 10 rounds/minute; 6–8 rounds/minute for aimed indirect fire from prepared positions and 4–6 rounds/minute for direct fire using HEAT rounds.

Left: *Nona*-K in service with Donetsk militiamen (almost certainly provided by Russia), November 2014. Right: Russian *Nona*-M1 in Ukraine, January 2024. Both can be used as traditional mortars, but only *Nona*-K is capable of direct fire. (Sem Dadazhe (YouTube); MORF)

Nona-S and its derivatives were intended to be 'universal' weapons capable of undertaking tasks traditionally assigned to guns, howitzers, and mortars, including direct fire against tanks. (MORF)

The 2A51's breech mechanism. The first breech block with obturator can be seen on the left, denoted by the red arrow. The second vertical-sliding breech block can be seen on the right. The loader must place the projectile inside the barrel such that the rear part is held by the retaining catch (yellow arrow) before operating the ramming system. (MORF)

The gunner uses the 1P8 combined sight for aiming. It consists of the direct-fire 1P30 telescopic sight and a mechanical sight with panoramic periscope for indirect fire. The round two-man turret nominally has a limited traverse arc of +/-35° and is operated manually. There is no turret basket, with the turret assembly not extending below the turret ring except for the crew seats. The loader and gunner occupy the turret, while the commander sits in the hull, to the driver's left. The fighting compartment contains the turret along with 25 rounds of ammunition. This was considered insufficient based on experience in the Soviet-Afghan War, and this was improved to 40 rounds (later, two hull-floor racks were reserved for *Kitolov*-2 PGMs), although only 25 rounds may be carried in the vehicle before an airdrop to keep weight at 8t.[20] Ammunition from an external source can also be passed into the vehicle via a rear hull hatch and a slide.

To minimise the vehicle's weight (8t; 8.5t for *Sviristelka*), armour protection is composed of rolled, welded ABT-101 aluminium alloy armour plating with a maximum thickness of 15mm on the hull and only 7mm on the turret. Radio equipment consists of the usual *Magnolia*-M VHF radio and *Lebed* crew intercom. VDV *Nona*-Ss are designed to work with the *Reostat* (1V119) artillery reconnaissance and fire direction vehicle, which is also based on the BTR-D.[21] It is rated to take no more than 0.5 minutes for a *Nona*-S to emplace/displace, though the time needed for a *Nona*-S battery (6x *Nona*-S + 2x *Reostat*) to open fire on an unplanned target after emplacing is 5–7 minutes. Modernised *Nona*-SMs have a computerised FCS, INS/SNS, telecode datalink, and *Arbalet* (R-163-60) radio complex. The *Reostat*-1 (1V119-1) modernisation also significantly overhauls the *Reostats* in a similar manner. As a result, the modernised battery has a shorter reaction time of 30–50 seconds.[22]

As mentioned previously, the *Nona*-S shares the same chassis as the BTR-D airborne APC: they have the same GBTU code (925). The most easily recognisable characteristic of the *Nona*-S and other members of the BMD family is their adjustable-ground clearance hydropneumatic suspension. These vehicles were intended to be carried and dropped by Soviet transport aircraft ranging from the large Ilyushin Il-76 and Antonov An-22 (comparable to the McDonnell Douglas C-17 Globemaster III) to the much smaller Antonov An-12 (comparable to the Lockheed C-130 Hercules). This imposed strict weight and size requirements, and the hydropneumatic suspension

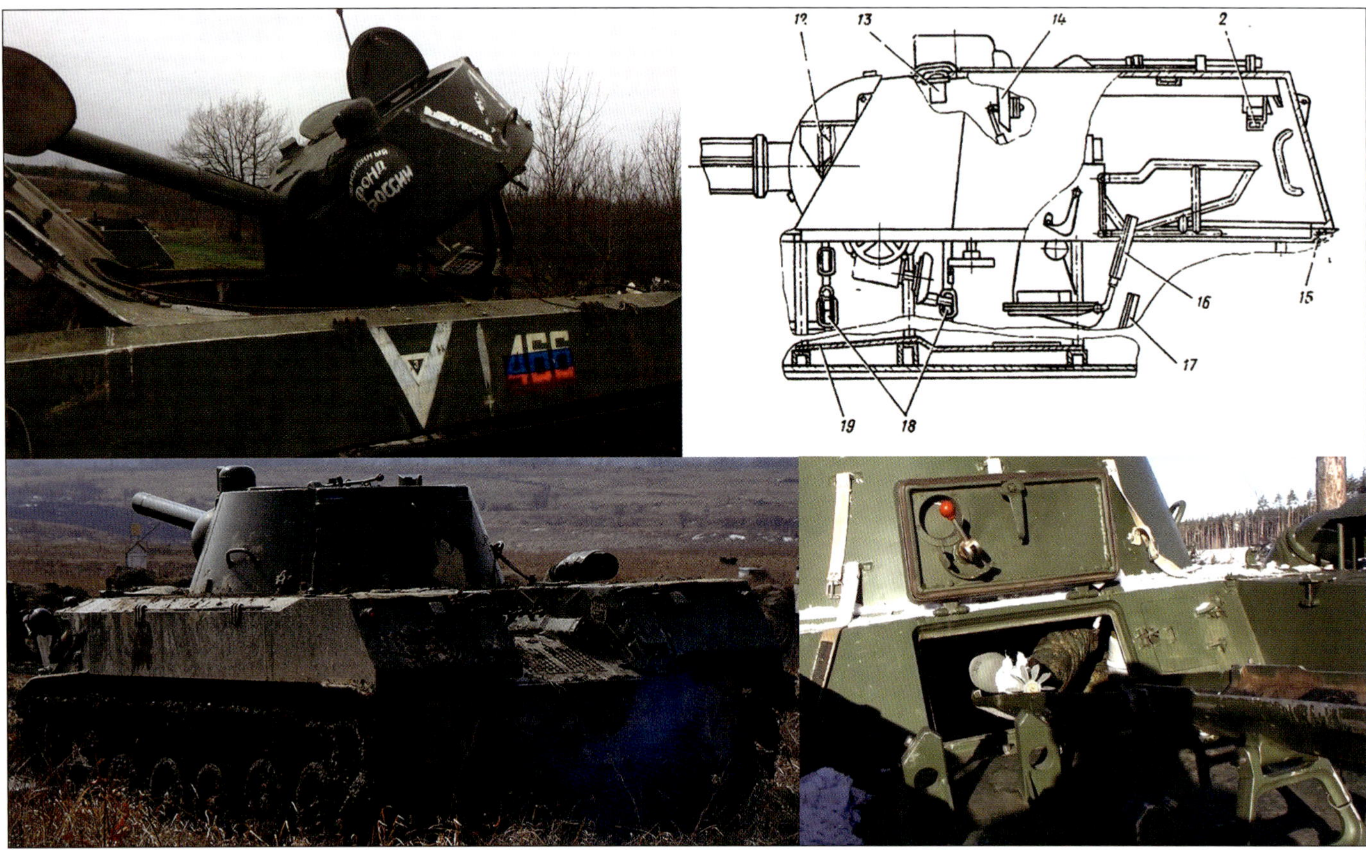

Top: Destroyed *Nona*-S of the 331st VDV Regiment in Nova Kakhovka, Ukraine, November 2022. A cutaway of the turret from the manual is shown on the right. *Nona*-S is highly vulnerable to anything more powerful than rifle-calibre bullets. Bottom: a view of a Nona-S's rear and the hull hatch and slide used to pass ammunition into the vehicle. (Top: Warspotting.net; author's collection; bottom: MORF)

allows the *Nona*-S's height to be reduced during transportation to a more compact size. It can also be used to raise height of the *Nona*-S in a firing position, allowing it to 'poke' out to fire before retracting back into cover, or to lower the hull until it touches the ground to help stability when firing. The vehicle can be driven at any clearance level. It is powered by a 240hp 5D20 V-6 diesel engine, providing a power/weight ratio of 30hp/t. The mechanical transmission has four forward and one reverse gear for a maximum speed of 60km/h. The *Nona*-S is also fully amphibious with minimal preparation. Airborne landings are carried out using the rocket-assisted PRSM-925 or unassisted PBS-925 parachute landing systems, which allow drops from relative altitudes of 300–1,500m to drop points up to 2,500m above sea level with ground wind speeds not exceeding 15m/s.

Context

The *Nona*-S provides a lot of firepower relative to its size: its rifled HE shell has an explosive filler between 122mm and 152mm shells, while the vehicle's mass is half that of *Gvozdika*. The mortar has a shorter range, but this is not seen as significant a weakness for the *Nona*-S in its intended role of providing indirect/direct fire support to the VDV during airborne operations. It even offers significantly more penetration (600mm RHA) and thus AT capability with its 3BK19 HEAT shell than its predecessors.[23] Thus, the 'universal weapon' would eventually entirely replace the Soviet VDV's SU-85s, 120mm regimental smoothbore mortars, and motorised guns, though not the D-30 howitzers. This was because the D-30 is more compact than either the *Nona*-S or the BM-21V MRL, has a longer

Nona-S's adjustable hydropneumatic suspension, as seen during the 2020 Slavic Brotherhood joint exercise. Right: illustration of the suspension from the BTR-D manual: the 'pneumatic spring' (17) functions as both a shock absorber and vehicle hull clearance adjuster by adjusting the air pressure within the lower cylinder using the hydraulic piston above it. Track tension is adjusted by a hydraulic piston (2) connected to the front idler wheel. (MORF; author's collection)

Left: *Nona*-S of the 25th 'Sicheslav' Airborne Brigade near Kreminna, Luhansk, summer 2023. The long-term serviceability of Ukrainian *Nona*-Ss is doubtful due to lack of spares. Right: Captured Nona-SVK in Ukrainian service near Izium, September 2022, formerly of the Russian 752nd Motor-Rifle Regiment. (25 Airborne; Radnuli (YouTube))

range than the former and is also a much more accurate weapon than the latter, and thus still filled a niche.[24]

The VDV are often used as the primary rapid response and power projection force of today's Russian Federation, and have thus been heavily engaged in the various conflicts Russia has been involved in since 1991. As the VDV's primary heavy fire support weapon, the *Nona*-S is thus an indispensable part of their arsenal, providing much needed mobility and firepower. Ironically, though, the *Nona*-S's airdrop capability has never been used in any of the wars the Russian VDV has been deployed to.[25] It is estimated that Russia had 279 *Nona*-S/SVKs in 2013 across all branches of service. In addition to modernising the *Nonas*, the Russians have also been interested in ultimately replacing the 122mm calibre within other parts of their military with the 120mm. This has led to developments such as the *Vena* (GRAU: 2S31) based on the BMP-3 chassis and *Khosta* (see *Gvozdika* section), but these have not seen widespread adoption. In November 2023, it was reported that yet another iteration of the 'universal weapon', *Floks* (GRAU: 2S40), was put into Russian service. A wheeled SPG based on the Ural-4320 6x6 truck chassis, whether the *Floks* will see widespread adoption within the Russian military is an open question, though it has been deployed in combat in Ukraine.[26] *Nona*-S itself is intended to be replaced by the *Lotos* (GRAU: 2S42), based on the BMD-4M, but the system is still undergoing trials at the time of writing. It is unlikely that the *Nona*-S will be completely replaced in the near future, and the place of the versatile 120mm rifled mortar in the Russian arsenal also seems assured for the immediate and long-term future.

Ukraine is known to have inherited a small number of *Nona*-Ss, estimated by Zhirokhov at ~50. With the exception of three sold to China, by 2014 they had been consolidated into the 25th 'Sicheslav' Airborne Brigade, which is also the only Ukrainian unit to still operate BMDs. They saw combat during the Donbas War phase of the Russo-Ukrainian War, but attrition from usage has dwindled their numbers in service. This is because manufacture of the chassis and its spares was centred in Volgograd, today part of Russia, which has made maintaining the vehicle in Ukrainian service difficult, especially the hydropneumatic suspension.[27] It is fairly unlikely that more than a handful of these *Nona*-S's are still in service at the time of writing. To get around this problem, the Ukrainians have resurrected the *Nona*-SV project mating the *Nona*-S turret to the BMP-1/2 chassis, of which at least four are known to have been converted. This conversion would be much easier for the Ukrainians keep operational, as they have the infrastructure to maintain BMPs.[28]

There is no direct Western equivalent to the *Nona*-S, as the role it plays in the VDV does not really exist in Western militaries due to differences in doctrine. However, since the end of the Cold War some systems have appeared that might be considered comparable. These include the Polish *Rak* SP mortar, which is currently used in limited numbers by the ZSU. Like the *Nona*-S, the *Rak* can conduct both direct and indirect fire. Its turret can be mounted on tracked (SMG120) or wheeled (SMK120) chassis. However, the *Rak* uses a smoothbore mortar and is an altogether more advanced design from the 2000s, having sophisticated computerised fire control and an automatic loader. It is also not meant to be airdroppable and is intended to support Polish battalion combat teams, more akin to the *Nona*-SV/SVK.[29]

8
MSTA: THE NEXT GENERATION

Development History

In 1976, development of a new 152mm howitzer was officially initiated under Sergeev's leadership at *Barrikady*'s OKB-2. Named after the Msta River in northwestern Russia, the new *Msta dupleks* would follow the *Giatsint*'s pattern with the towed (*Msta*-B) and SP (*Msta*-S) parts developed roughly contemporaneously.[1] As was typical, OKB-2 would develop the *Msta*-B (GRAU: 2A65) as well as the SPG's ordnance (GRAU: 2A64), while Uraltransmash's OKB-3 was assigned development of the *Msta*-S vehicle (GRAU: 2S19; GBTU: 316) in 1980, now under Tomashov. It may come as a surprise that the Soviets would develop a new 152mm family so soon after the *Akatsiya* and *Giatsints* had entered service; to understand why, one must take a look at developments occurring on the other side of the Iron Curtain.

Ukrainian *Msta*-S of 26 Art., November 2020. This was the only known Ukrainian unit to operate the type in significant numbers prior to 2022. (MOU)

Ukrainian *Msta*-B towed howitzer of Operational-Tactical Group 'Mariupol', Donetsk region, October 2017. *Msta*-B is considerably more common in Ukrainian service than its SP counterpart. (MOU)

The 1970s had brought significant advancements to NATO artillery arsenals, one of the most important of which was the introduction of a 155mm L/39 barrel on the American M109A1, the standard SPG found in most NATO armies. This allowed the M109A1 to match its Soviet 152mm counterparts, the *Akatsiya* SPG and towed D-20 howitzer, in terms of range. In addition to conventional rounds, the M109A1 was also capable of firing XM454 AFAP (Artillery Fired Atomic Projectile) tactical nuclear shells, while its extended range meant that the standard Soviet 152mm divisional artillery could no longer counter the M109A1 as effectively. The M109's tactical nuclear capabilities' impact on the *Msta*'s design can be seen in the list of intended tasks present in the *Msta*-B/S manuals, the very first of which specifies 'destruction of the enemy's tactical means of nuclear attack'. Furthermore, other advanced NATO artillery systems were also in the development pipeline, such as the French AUF1 and Anglo-German-Italian SP70 and FH70, all of which promised to be even more capable with ranges of around 24km using standard HE-Frag and exceeding 30km using RAP.

To meet these threats, the GRAU issued requirements for a new 152mm divisional howitzer that could achieve similar ranges. It was further intended that the new howitzer would eventually replace not only the divisional 152mm howitzers, but all the various calibres then in Soviet service from 122mm to 203mm, mirroring similar NATO nations' moves consolidating around 155mm as their primary artillery calibre to simplify logistics. While the *Giatsints* could attain the ranges desired, they could only do so using high-powered 152mm ammunition specially designed for them and at the cost of reduced barrel life. The new *Mstas* were required to be compatible with the full range of 152mm ammunition developed for older *Akatsiyas*, D-20s, and ML-20s, including nuclear shells. Great attention was paid to improving the accuracy of the new howitzers, both in terms of the aerodynamic design of the new long-range projectiles and the gun stability when firing. The *Msta*-S SPG's chassis was also required to be unified with that of the next-generation Soviet MBTs then entering mass production. It would also have to be capable of using both internally and externally supplied ammunition without any loss in rate-of-fire.

Development of the towed *Msta*-B proceeded relatively straightforwardly and it entered service first in 1986. As for the *Msta*-S SPG, originally it had been intended to use the T-72 MBT's chassis as its basis. However, during testing of the first prototypes in 1985–86, KB-3 encountered unsolvable problems with dispersion due to the rocking of the chassis when firing. This is likely a result of the T-72 having the 'stiffest' suspension among the next-generation Soviet MBTs (T-64, T-72, and T-80).[2] Thus, KB-3 instead developed a 'hybrid' chassis, utilising the basic hull geometry, engine, and transmission of the T-72 combined with the suspension components of the T-80. Turret development was subcontracted to the innocuously named 'Instrument Design Bureau' (*Konstruktorskoye byuro priboristroeniya*, KBP) based in Tula. In order to mass produce the *Msta*-S, it was planned to expand Uraltransmash's production capacity with a complete reconstruction of their Sverdlovsk factory, but this was not planned to be completed until 1995. Thus, a second production facility was built in Sterlitamak in neighbouring Bashkortostan (Bashkiria), which began production at the end of 1988. Following tests, the *Msta*-S was accepted into service in 1989. The official test report concluded: '"*Msta*-S" can become the basis for a new generation of domestic field artillery'.[3]

In addition to the basic *Msta*-B and *Msta*-S, since 1991 several variant of the *Msta*-S have been developed and put into service in significant numbers:

- *Msta*-SM1 (GRAU: 2S19M1): *Uspekh* (1V168) automated artillery FCS and GLONASS SNS. Adopted 2008; modernisation of existing *Msta*-S's.
- *Msta*-SM2 (GRAU: 2S19M2): 152mm 2A64M2, BMS with GLONASS SNS integration, increased rate-of-fire, and 1V169-1 FCS with multiple rounds simultaneous impact (MRSI) capability. Adopted 2013; new-build vehicles.

The term '*Msta*-SM' is also sometimes used to refer to either of these variants, but this can lead to confusion with the '*Msta*-SM' (GRAU: 2S33) deep modernisation project, which was cancelled in favour of the prospective next-generation *Koalitsiya*-SV sometime in the 2000s. The following technical summaries will focus on the basic *Msta*-B and *Msta*-S variants, as these are the ones to which the author has access to detailed information. Significant differences in capability introduced by the modernised versions will be noted where necessary.

Technical Summary (Msta-B)

The *Msta*-B towed howitzer has a 152mm L/53 monobloc barrel (including muzzle brake), significantly longer than the D-20's L/34 barrel and comparable to the *Giatsint*-B's. This is capped by a triple baffle muzzle brake, dissipating up to 63 percent of the recoil. In order to achieve the required range, a new long-range HE-Frag projectile designated 3OF45 *Namestnik*-1 was developed specifically for the *Mstas*. *Namestnik*-1 has a longer, more streamlined profile than previous 152mm shells and is the first Soviet 'hollow-base' shell, featuring a tapered aerodynamic ring screwed on to the base of the shell. The ring reduces the base drag induced by turbulent vortices at the base of the shell. With the special 4Zh61 long-range charge, the *Msta*-B can throw the 43.6kg *Namestnik*-1 at 810m/s out to 24.7km. This can be extended to 28.9km using the 3OF61 *Alagez* base bleed (BB) shell. As noted previously, the *Mstas* were also required to be fully compatible with older 152mm divisional howitzer ammunition: the range achieved with the D-20/*Akatsiya*'s *Grif* HE-Frag shell and 4Zh38 charge is 17.8km, slightly further than when fired from the older weapons.

Top: *Msta*-SM1 of the Russian 15th Guards Motor-Rifle Regiment practices direct fire, November 2020. *Msta*-SM1 can be distinguished from the base *Msta*-S by the presence of an SNS antenna next to the tall radio antenna. Bottom: *Msta*-SM2s of the 99th SP Artillery Regiment practice driving in column prior to the Victory Day Parade, April 2019. The most reliable way to identify the *Msta*-SM2 is its 152mm 2A64M2 gun, which has a longer right recoil cylinder: on previous variants, the cylinders are of equal length. (MORF)

Ukrainian *Msta*-B 'Margo' firing at Russian forces on the Zaporizhzhia front, June 2022. Although 155mm pieces like the M777 have mostly taken over as the ZSU's primary calibre, it was 152mm pieces like the *Msta*-B that played the crucial role in blunting the early stages of the Russian invasion. (ArmyInform)

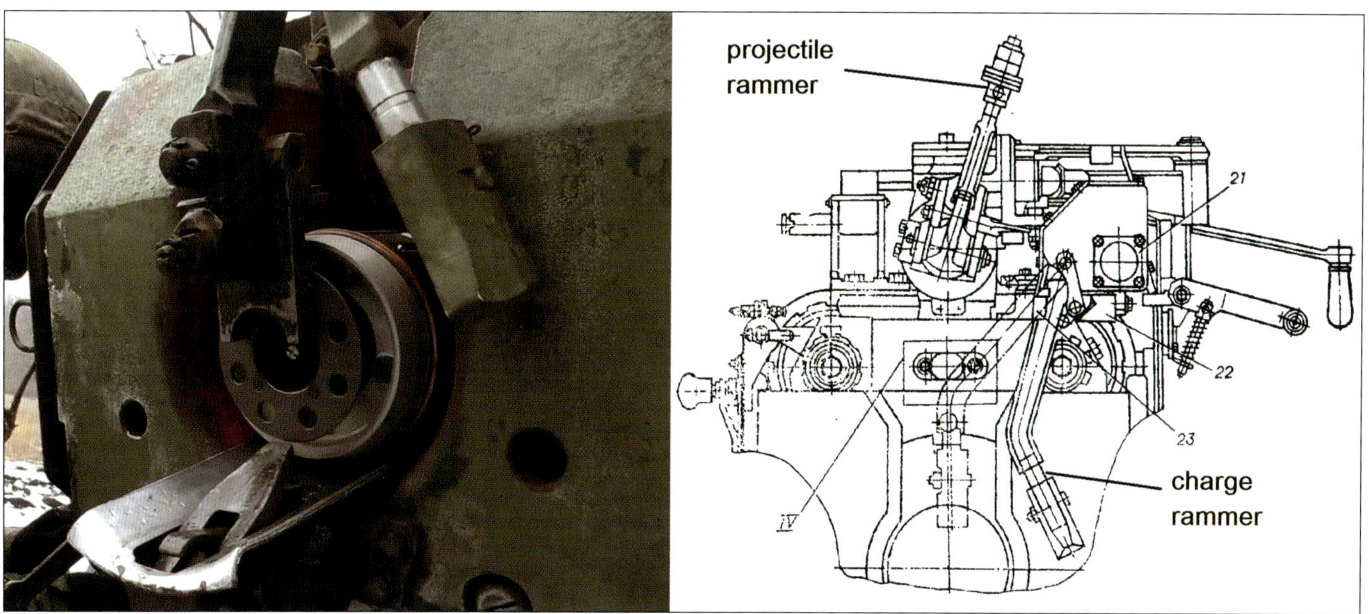

Msta-B can use two spring-loaded rammers to ram projectiles and charges into the bore. The projectile is first placed in the tray and its rammer is swung down into the loading line, as seen on the left with a *Krasnopol* laser-guided PGM being loaded into a Russian Pacific Fleet Marines *Msta*-B somewhere in Ukraine, January 2023. Once the projectile is loaded, the rammer automatically swings out of the way, and the process is repeated for the charge using the other rammer. They are rarely seen in use. (MORF; author's collection)

As with the D-20 and *Giatsint*-B, a vertical-sliding block breech is used. To assist the gunners and increase the rate-of-fire, particular when loading at high elevation angles, two spring-loaded rammers are provided. One is used to ram the projectile into the barrel and the other is used to ram the charge in after the projectile. Both rammers are cocked by the recoil from firing, thus the first shot with the howitzer must be loaded manually. The maximum rate-of-fire is seven rounds/minute. Indirect fire aiming is conducted using a mechanical sight with the standard PG-1M panoramic periscope. The primary type used is the Sb 00-19/BM-21 which, as the name might suggest, is the same as on the BM-21 *Grad* MRL, but the manual also allows for the older D-726-45/PG-1M. As usual, provision is also given for an OP4M-97K direct fire telescopic sight. The *Msta*-B has a maximum elevation of 70°, allowing it to lob shells in high-arcing trajectories that were previously impossible with the D-20, and +/-27.5° of horizontal traverse. The elevation and traverse gears have two speed settings: a regular speed for normal aiming, and a fast mode for quickly getting the gun aimed in the rough bearing and elevation.

The *Msta*-B's two-wheel split-trail carriage design is fairly conventional and resembles the D-20's. Like the D-20, it employs a pedestal jack and trail rollers for stability and rapidly changing the firing direction of the gun. A shield is also provided to give some modicum of protection to the crew and gun mechanisms, a feature that has long since disappeared from most Western towed guns. Pneumatic tires and a torsion bar suspension allow for high-speed towing on roads at up to 80km/h. The entire weapon is considerably heavier than the D-20, weighing 7t. The manual gives the time taken to bring the *Msta*-B into or out of action at 2–2.5 minutes. The specified crew comprises eight personnel.

Russian *Msta*-B of the 3rd Motor-Rifle Division, 20th Guards Combined Arms Army, September 2018. Some important devices are helpfully marked in red: the red buttons on the elevation/traverse gears are the speed settings, seen in the left picture. On the right, the upper handle is for re-cocking the firing pin without opening the breech during a misfire, while the lower handle is the firing lever for firing the gun. The projectile rammer is also marked in red, stowed in the raised position. The Sb 00-19/BM-21 mechanical and OP4M-97K telescopic sights are also clearly visible. (MORF)

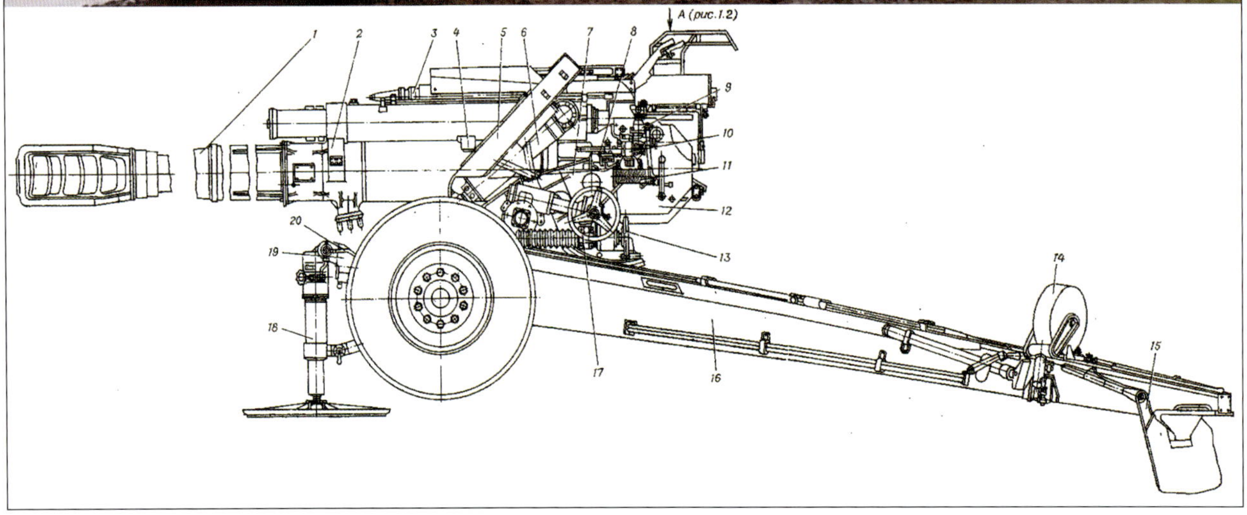

Top: the KamAZ-63501AT *Medved* ('Bear') 8x8 artillery tractor is the VSRF's dedicated prime mover for the *Msta*-B. Introduced in 2009, it features a six-passenger compartment in the middle along with the two-person driver's cabin, allowing it to carry an entire gun crew with NBC and GOST Class 5 (7.62mm bulletproof) protection. Bottom: illustration of a deployed *Msta*-B from the manual, showing the pedestal jack. (MORF; author's collection)

Technical Summary (*Msta*-S)

Msta-S's 152mm 2A64 howitzer is ballistically identical to *Msta*-B, distinguished mainly by the presence of a fume extractor to reduce gas build-up in the SPG during prolonged firing. The breech is mated to a fairly complex combined rammer/case ejection mechanism. The latter is a first for Soviet SPGs, as previous ones simply relied on the loader throwing out spent charge cases from a nearby hatch. Loading of most projectiles can be done completely automatically with the mechanised conveyor racks, the breech rammer's side projectile loading tray, and their associated chain rammers. However, due to their greater length, *Krasnopol* laser-guided PGMs must be loaded manually. The loaders must transfer charges by hand into the breech rammer, either placing it in the top loading tray or directly into the rammer.

All ammunition is stored inside the massive slab-sided turret. The maximum number of complete rounds that can be carried is 50: 46 regular projectiles can be stored in two 23-round mechanised conveyor racks, with another four at the ends of the racks located within the frames of each conveyor. Up to seven PGMs like *Krasnopol* can be carried, although they must be stored in two pieces and assembled before loading due to their greater length, and will thus reduce the number of regular projectiles that can be carried by

Ukrainian *Msta*-S of 26 Art. firing during what the Ukrainians euphemistically call the 'anti-terrorist operation' phase of the Russo–Ukrainian War, ca. 2015. (26 Art.)

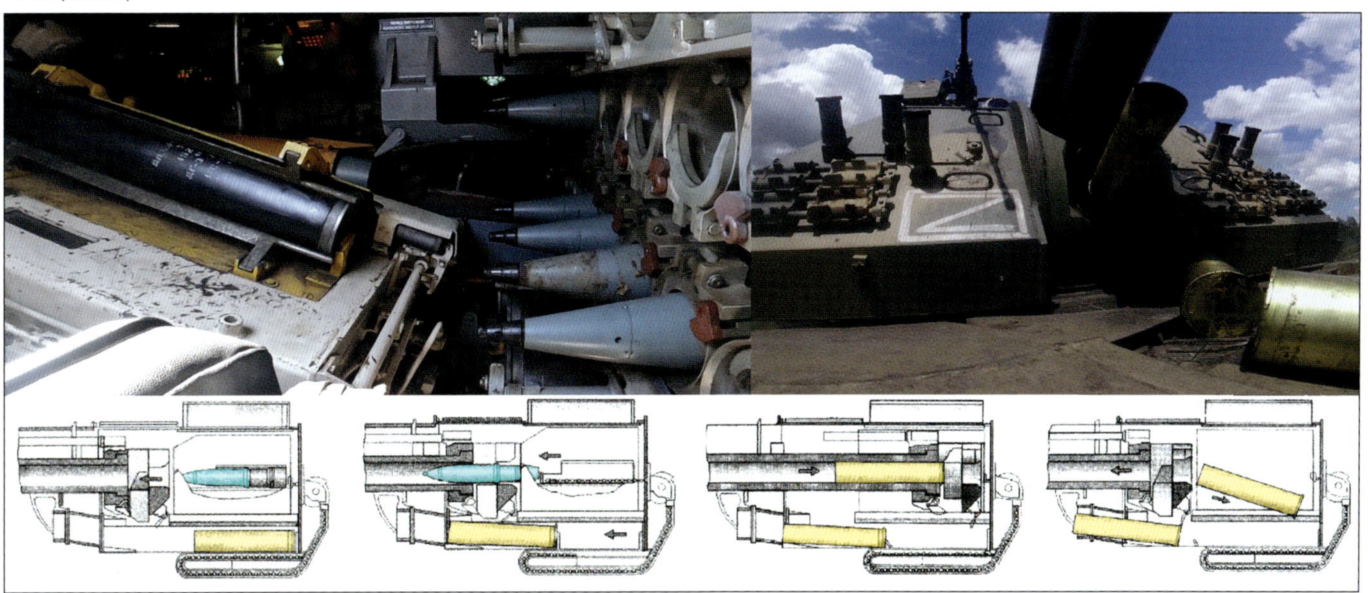

Top: the breech rammer/case ejector can be seen on the left. Projectiles can be automatically fed from the two mechanised projectile conveyor racks into the loading tray on the right of the breech. Charges are placed manually by a loader on the top loading tray: here, a 4Zh61 long-range charge can be seen in its distinctive black prefabricated plastic case. Spent cases are ejected from a port underneath the gun barrel, as seen on the right. Bottom: sequence from a manual depicting the loading and ejection process. (MORF; author's collection)

Top: the *Msta*-SM2's external conveyor for projectiles can be seen in use here along with the hatch for charges. When not in use, the conveyor is stowed in a folded position, as seen on the right. Bottom: diagrams from a manual illustrating the ammunition stowage, internal conveyor racks, and the external ammunition feed system. (MORF; author's collection)

11. As with the *Akatsiya*, *Msta*-S also has provisions for firing using externally supplied ammunition: in fact, according to the manual, this is supposed to be the 'main operating mode' for the SPG.[4] An external conveyor system is provided for feeding shells from outside the SPG into the bottom internal conveyor racks, which can then be fed automatically into the breech rammer via the side loader. Charges are loaded from outside using a separate conveyor via a hatch on the lower left side of the turret, where they are then picked up by one of the loaders. The maximum rate-of-fire given in the manual is 7–8 rounds/minute. The *Msta*-SM2 has an improved loading system allowing for up to 10 rounds/minute.

In addition to the howitzer, *Msta*-S has a remote-controlled mounting fitted a 12.7mm *Utyos* (NSVT) AAMG on the commander's cupola for close protection against infantry or aircraft. It is similar in design to the mounting used on the T-64A/B and T-80UD/84 MBTs, and 300 rounds are carried. The cupola also has the standard commander's TKN-3V combined day/night sight and OU-3GKU IR searchlight. For aiming the howitzer itself, the basic *Msta*-S has the 1P22 sighting complex for indirect fire and its integrated 1P23 direct fire telescopic sight. The 1P22 has a panoramic periscope and can be used for manual aiming, but it is primarily intended to be used in automatic mode in partnership with the 1V122 data receiver and 2E46 turret traverse and gun elevation drive as a part of the 1V124 complex. 1V122 receives firing coordinates and data (charge amount, fuse settings, sight angle, gun angle settings, etc.) from the 1V518-1 transmitter on 1V13M battery platoon command vehicles of the *Faltset* complex. The 1P122 sighting complex then sets the gun automatically to the required angles.

On *Msta*-SM1s, the 1V124 system was replaced by the *Uspekh* digital automated FCS and 2E46M turret drive, integrated with a *Grot*-V (14Ts821) SNS to further speed up fire control. *Msta*-SM2s have the 1V169-1 FCS with a colour digital map display and 2E46M2 traverse/elevation drive with MRSI capability: firing multiple rounds quickly at different elevations automatically so that they impact the target simultaneously.[5] Compared to the basic *Msta*-S/*Faltset* combination, *Msta*-SM1/2s with the modernised *Mashina*-M (1V12-3) artillery fire control complex greatly reduced the time taken to open fire after receiving an order while on the march (10–12 minute vs. 3–3.5 minute) and to fire on an unplanned target (4.5–5.5 minute vs. 30–50 seconds).[6] This finally put Russian artillery fire control on a comparable footing with Western counterparts.The basic *Msta*-S uses the Soviet R-173 radio; *Msta*-SM1/SM2 replaced this with the *Akveduk* (R-168) radio complex, standard for modern Russian military vehicles.[7]

Automotively, the *Msta*-S is a hybrid of the T-72 and T-80 MBTs, somewhat akin to the *Pion*. The engine on the base *Msta*-S is the 780hp V-84A V-12 diesel engine, while the *Msta*-SM1/SM2 have improved 780hp V-84AMS engines.[8] *Msta*-S weighs 42t, giving a power/weight ratio of 18.6hp/t, while the *Msta*-SM2 is slightly heavier at 43.2t.[9] The transmission is of the BKP type used on the T-72, with seven forward and one reverse gear providing a top road speed of 60km/h. The road wheels, torsion bar suspension, tracks, and telescoping shock absorbers are from the T-80. In addition to the engine, a 16 kW AP-18D gas turbine APU is fitted in the turret to allow operating electrical systems for extended periods without the engine running.

The basic hull geometry is derived from that of the T-72, and it is configured much like a classic MBT is, with front driver, middle turret fighting, and rear engine compartments. However, while the imposing size and tank-like configuration of the *Msta*-S might suggest it is heavily armoured, this is far from reality: the hull armour is only made of 15mm RHA steel plating.[10] There are six smoke grenade launchers of the 902B *Tucha* ('Cloud') system on the turret front, and the *Msta*-S can also produce smoke screen by injecting fuel into the exhaust manifold; both features not found on other Soviet SPGs but common on Soviet MBTs. A manually

Left: the commander's cupola with OU-3GKU IR searchlight and remote-controlled *Utyos* AAMG. The armoured hood for the 1P22's panoramic sight is on the right. Right: 1P22 sight. The left eyepiece is for the 1P22's panoramic periscope, while the right one is for the 1P23 direct fire telescopic sight. (MORF)

lowered dozer blade, similar to that found on the T-72, is also provided on the hull's lower glacis. The total crew is five, comprising driver, gunner, commander, and two loaders. When operating using externally supplied ammunition, another two personnel are required to handle the ammunition outside in addition to the five within the SPG. It is rated to take no more than two minutes for the *Msta*-S to emplace/displace.

Context

In terms of most key parameters such as range and rate-of-fire, the *Mstas* were fairly comparable with contemporary Western artillery pieces. The *Msta*-B is relatively simple compared to Western towed pieces like the French 155 TRF1 and Anglo-German-Italian FH70: it lacks features like an APU for limited SP capability and hydraulically assisting with moving the trails, powered elevation/traverse gear, digital displays, or burst firing capability using a flick rammer. Gunners used to the D-20, however, would probably not find themselves missing any of those features. The *Msta*-S, on the other hand, is a significantly more advanced machine than the preceding *Akatsiya*. In the 1980s, its closest NATO equivalent would have been the French AUF1, which was very similar in performance and capabilities. However, most NATO armies at the time would have been relegated to the American M109A3/A4, which was substantially disadvantaged in terms of range and rate-of-fire.

The *Mstas* were the last, and thus most advanced, towed and SP guns to enter service with the Soviet Army. They began to replace the older D-20/*Akatsiyas* as the standard divisional howitzers of Soviet tank/motor-rifle divisions, but the USSR's collapse in 1991 put paid to the ambitious plan of replacing all other Soviet artillery calibres. Only approximately 1,200 *Msta*-Bs and 500 *Msta*-S's had been produced by 1991, which was completely insufficient to replace even the existing fleet of 152mm towed and SP guns (e.g. there were already ~1,200 *Giatsint*-Bs alone at the time). The bulk of this fleet and the production facilities were inherited by Russia. The Sterlitamak factory was closed after 1991 as it was cheaper to build them in Sverdlovsk, but even production at the latter was reduced to a tiny trickle for most of the 1990s and early 2000s as Russian funding dried up.[11]

Production of the *Msta*-S has picked up somewhat since the late 2000s: by 2019, the anonymous military blogger 'Altyn73' deduced (based on photographic evidence of the number of Russian units equipped with *Msta*-S's) that the total number in service was ~730, which by their reckoning would make it not only the most common artillery piece in the VSRF service but also the third most common Russian AFV after the T-72 MBT and BMP-2 IFV. Of these, 260 were modernised *Msta*-SM1s and 180 were new-build *Msta*-SM2s.[12] It is thus not surprising that the *Msta*-S has been the workhorse Russian artillery piece of the Russo-Ukrainian War. This is reflected in the losses suffered as documented by Oryxspioenkop, which amount to over 250 *Msta*-Ss

Left: an excellent study of the Msta-S suspension with side skirts removed. The Msta-S is somewhat rear-heavy, thus the road wheels are more closely spaced towards the rear of the vehicle to better support the heavy turret and engine compartment. Like the T-72, the Msta-S's exhaust is on the left side of the vehicle. Right: the AP-18D APU located on the rear right side of the turret and the impressive flame jet produced on start-up. (ArmyInform; MORF)

Ukrainian *Msta*-B of 55 Art. firing near Pervomaisk, Luhansk, July 2014. Alongside D-30s, *Msta*-Bs formed the bulk of the Ukrainian towed artillery in service at the beginning of the war. (Informator)

at the time of writing, the highest of any Russian SPG. The *Msta*-B also occupies a similar place among Russian towed artillery, with at least 120 lost. *Mstas* are commonly paired with the *Orlan*-10 UAS, and together they are a highly effective and deadly combination due in part to the improved efficiency and accuracy that UAS spotting provides as well as the sheer numbers of both systems that have been available so far.[13]

Ukraine is known to have inherited 40 *Msta*-S's and 185 *Msta*-Bs from the USSR. In 2014, the SPGs were used exclusively by the 26th 'Roman Dashkevich' Artillery Brigade, which had two divisions with 18 SPGs each.[14] The *Msta*-Bs in service were concentrated in the 55th 'Zaporizka Sich' Artillery Brigade, which was initially only able to field a single battery of six guns out of an on-paper strength of 18. This battery was heavily committed during the Donbas War stage of the Russo-Ukrainian War, particularly in the battles for Sloviansk and Debaltseve, on occasion firing up to 600 shells/day. More *Msta*-Bs were reactivated to equip newly established artillery brigades throughout 2014–2015, with 102 in service by December 2015.[15] Since 2022, 26 Art. has reequipped with the *Krab* and PzH 2000 SPGs and appears to have retired its *Msta*-S's, based on a lack of appearances in their social media. However, Ukraine is also known to have captured at least 52 *Msta*-S's, and at least one ex-Russian *Msta*-SM2 is currently being used by the 95th Polesian Air Assault Brigade.[16] *Msta*-Bs remain in service, although their long-term future is uncertain as Ukraine will likely eventually transition to the NATO 155mm standard.

During the 1990s, Western artillery design leapfrogged ahead with 155mm L/45 and L/52 pieces whose ranges exceed 30km while firing standard projectiles along with advances in automated fire control. Despite several proposed modernisation programmes over the decades, Russian improvements to the *Mstas* have so far been limited to greater command and fire control automation. It seems that more focus has been placed on developing the planned successor to *Msta*-S: *Koalitsiya*-SV. However, *Koalitsiya*-SV's development has suffered significant delays and it was only at the end of 2023 that the first production examples were delivered to the VSRF. It is highly unlikely that *Koalitsiya*-SV will replace the *Msta* family in the near future, and indeed there is no visual evidence they have been sent into combat in Ukraine at the time of writing. While they do not have the range or sophistication of the latest Western systems being sent to Ukraine like CAESAR or PzH 2000, the *Mstas* are available in far greater numbers and are one of the biggest contributing factors to the significant weight-of-fire advantage that Russia has consistently enjoyed so far in the war. They are thus not to be underestimated.

Russian *Msta*-SM2s operating in Ukraine, March and July 2023. They are the most advanced Russian SPGs used in significant numbers during the invasion and will likely remain so for the foreseeable future. (MORF)

KOALITSIYA & *MALVA*

Koalitsiya-SV (GRAU: 2S35) is the prospective Russian response to modern NATO 155mm L/52 SPGs like PzH 2000. Its origins date back to 2002, when the Burevestnik design bureau began work on a multipurpose combat modular turret for potentially unifying land and naval artillery systems. The new turret was to be armed with a twin-barrel 152mm 2A86 L/52 gun (hence '*Koalitsiya*' — 'Coalition' [of two guns];[17] 'SV' — 'ground forces'), where loading of both barrels would be done automatically in one cycle to dramatically increase the rate-of-fire. However, a single-barrel version was also developed and tested; the twin-barrel concept was eventually abandoned in favour of a more reliable and (more importantly) cheaper single-barrel SPG in 2006. Despite this change, the name was retained for the 'downsized' system, and the first prototypes were completed by Uraltransmash in 2013, with the system making its first public appearance in the 2015 Victory Day parade.[18] However, state tests would not be completed for another decade, with the first delivery to the VSRF only announced in January 2024.[19]

Much like with the Russian *Armata* future combat vehicle programme, relatively little is solidly known about *Koalitsiya*-SV and most of what is known is based on Russian mass media reports. Its 152mm 2A88 L/52 gun is claimed to have a maximum range of 70km (presumably with extended-range ammunition) and a rate-of-fire of up to 16 rounds/minute, achieved with the help of liquid-cooling. This is a potentially massive increase in firepower compared to existing systems like *Msta*-SM2, but to achieve this, *Koalitsiya*-SV is believed to use modular charges (like modern Western SPGs) coupled with an autoloader in an unmanned turret.[20] No other Russian 152mm artillery piece uses such charges, and the *Koalitsiya*-SV would also be completely incompatible with older metal-cased charges. Thus, the ammunition supply infrastructure would have to be completely revamped and the charge stockpile also manufactured from scratch to properly support the *Koalitsiya*-SV. This is a difficult challenge even in peacetime, and would be an absurd proposition while Russia is fighting the war with Ukraine. This, combined with the small number built so far, is probably why there has not been a confirmed combat sighting of *Koalitsiya*-SV. It is possible the *Koalitsiya* has been used in small-scale combat trials in Ukraine, but there is no visual evidence of this at the time of writing.

On the other side of the complexity spectrum is *Malva* (GRAU: 2S43), one of the newest Russian artillery systems to be adopted. Also developed by Burevestnik, *Malva* is a wheeled artillery system very similar in concept and layout to the French CAESAR.[21] It is basically made of the *Msta*-S's 152mm 2A64 gun in an exposed mounting at the rear of a BAZ-6010-27 8x8 truck. It appears to retain the breech assembly of the 2A64 with its semi-automatic loading system for projectiles and charges, and is claimed to have a rate-of-fire of seven rounds/minute. Like CAESAR, it is equipped with an automatic gun-laying system.[22] It is not known if the crew must dismount in order to fire the gun, though loading must certainly be done from outside the vehicle, as the projectiles and charges are stored in boxes next to the gun. It offers many of the same advantages (and disadvantages) of the CAESAR, being significantly lighter (32t vs. 42t) and more road-mobile than the *Msta*-S tracked SPG, but with the inherent limitations of wheeled vehicles cross-country. However, since it still uses the *Msta*'s gun, it is inferior to CAESAR in range.

It is not publicly known at the time of writing when development of the system began, though the first images of it appeared online in 2019. After several years of testing, *Malva* entered service with the VSRF in October 2023 and the system was first visually sighted in combat in June 2024.[23] The extensive use of existing components promises to significantly cut production time and costs, and *Malva* can also be more seamlessly integrated into the existing VSRF logistical infrastructure than *Koalitsiya*-SV since it uses the same gun and ammunition as the *Msta*-S, even if it is a much less capable system on paper. It can therefore be expected that more *Malvas* will be seen in combat in Ukraine in the future.

There has also been speculation that the *Koalitsiya*-SV's 2A88 gun could be mounted on the *Malva*, though this would again run into the same logistical problem with the modular charges and no physical prototype of this sort has been seen at the time of writing. More recently, a variant using the older *Giatsint*-B's ordnance has also been sighted in Ukraine; it is designated '*Giatsint*-K', though its claimed GRAU index 2S44 clearly ties it to the *Malva*.[24] [25] *Malva*'s design makes accommodating different guns on the chassis a relatively simple affair, though whether the appearance of this model is a sign that Russian *Msta* barrel production is unable to keep up with frontline demands remains to be seen.

Left: *Malva* at the 'Army 2024' exhibition in Russia, August 2024. Right: *Koalitsiya*-SV seen during a Victory Day parade rehearsal in Moscow, May 2018. ('Nickel Nitride'; Dmitriy Fomin, Wikimedia)

APPENDIX 1: PROJECTILES

The following are lists of projectiles for the various artillery calibres described in the book. These lists are not comprehensive and are mostly restricted to HE, cluster, and guided munitions used for indirect fire missions. They do not include other munitions such as direct-fire AT, smoke, leaflet, illumination, electronic countermeasures etc.

Left: Training cutaway model of 3OF45 *Namestnik*-1 HE shell with RGM-2 point-detonating fuse and G-540 brass propellant charge container. The hollow base of the shell can be seen clearly the GRAU has separate indices for projectiles and charges, as well as the projectile and charge combination. For example, the complete round of 3OF45 + RGM-2 + 4Zh38 (4B38 full propellant charge filling + G-540 brass case) has its own index 3VOF58. This combination is rated for use only with the *Msta* artillery family, although the 4Zh38 charge was inherited from the older D-20/*Akatsiya* and ML-20. Right: F-864 mortar bomb being hoisted aboard a *Tyulpan*. The additional propellant bags have been tied around the tail. (26 Art.)

Weight of projectile includes the fuse unless otherwise noted, and may vary between individual shells depending on filling and manufacturing batch, thus should only be taken as a rough guide.

Shell lethality is a complex matter depending on many factors other than the explosive content and type, including angle of fall, projectile shape, and casing thickness, all of which can affect the fragmentation pattern. The filler content is provided only to give some idea of their relative effectiveness.

120mm

Only ammunition compatible with the Nona and RTF1 rifled mortars listed. Because of their common lineage, ammunition is interchangeable between these systems. Main charge within projectile tail with adjustable bagged charges tied (Soviet) or charge rings added to tail as needed. US/French ammunition has a slightly shorter range (~8km), and range is also shorter when firing Soviet fin-stabilised bombs (~7km). Projectile weight given as loaded without additional charges: the actual in-flight projectile mass is 15–16kg for most types, as the tail separates upon firing.

Table 2: 120mm Mortar Ammunition Characteristics

Name	Weight (kg)	Filler/Payload	Notes
3OF49	19.8	4.9kg A-IX-2	Soviet pre-rifled HE shell.
3OF50	19.8	3.25kg A-IX-2	Soviet pre-rifled HE RAP. 12.8km max range.
OE FMP 120 PRY F1	18.6	4.2kg TNT	French pre-rifled HE shell. Also known as PR14.
OE PAD FMP 120 PRY F2	18.6	2.7kg Comp. B	French pre-rifled HE RAP. Also known as PRPA. 13km max range.
HE M1101	~19	4.8kg PBXN-114	US pre-rifled HE shell based on French OE FMP 120 PRY F1.
3OF69 *Kitolov*-2	26	5.2kg HE	Russian laser-guided HE projectile with rudders for trajectory correction. Part of *Kitolov*-2 (2K28) complex. Intended for rifled 120mm mortars only.
OF-843B	16.2	1.4kg TD-50	Second World War Soviet fin-stabilised HE bomb for PM-38 mortar.
3OF5	15.6	1.25kg TD-50	Post-Second World War Soviet fin-stabilised HE bomb for PM-38 mortar.
3OF34/3OF36	16.1	3.43kg A-IX-2/ 3.16kg TA-80	1980s Soviet fin-stabilised HE bomb for 2B11 *Sani* mortar.

122mm

Only projectiles rated for D-30 and *Gvozdika* listed. Separate-loading ammunition with variable charges in brass or steel cases.

Table 3: 122mm artillery Ammunition Characteristics

Name	Weight (kg)	Filler/Payload	Notes
OF-462	21.8	3.7kg TNT	Second World War Soviet HE shell, inherited from M-30. Many variants with different shell construction.
3OF24 *Voron*	21.8	4kg A-IX-2	Post-Second World War Soviet HE shell.
3OF56 *Leshch*	21.8	4.4kg A-IX-2	1980s Soviet HE shell.

152mm

Soviet/Russian 152mm projectiles come in two separate families, one for D-20/*Akatsiya*/*Msta* guns, and the other for *Giatsint* guns. Ammunition is not considered interchangeable between the two families, especially the charges. Both families generally use separate-loading variable charge ammunition with brass/steel cases. *Msta* 4Zh61 long-range charges come in prefabricated plastic cases; they are not compatible with older howitzers. More recently, similar cases have also been seen for *Giatsint* ammunition.

Table 4: 152mm Artillery Ammunition Characteristics

Name	Weight (kg)	Filler/Payload	Notes
OF-540	43.6	~6kg TNT	Second World War Soviet HE, inherited from ML-20. Many variants with different shell construction.
3OF25 *Grif*	43.6	6.8kg A-IX-2	Post-Second World War Soviet HE.
3OF22 *Kren*	43.3	4.88kg A-IX-2	1970s Soviet HE RAP. 20.5km max range.
3OF39 *Krasnopol*	50.8	6.5kg A-IX-2	1980s Soviet laser-guided HE RAP with aerodynamic rudders for trajectory correction. Part of *Krasnopol* (2K25) PGM complex. 20km max range.
3OF39M *Krasnopol*-M	45	10kg A-IX-2	3OF39 with BB gas generator instead of rocket and improved laser-homing head. Part of *Krasnopol*-M (2K25M) PGM complex. 25km max range.
3O13 *Sakharoza*	41.4	8 x 3O16	1980s Soviet cluster munitions shell. Each 3O16 fragmentation submunition contains 0.23kg A-IX-2. 14km max range.
3OF45 *Namestnik*-1	43.6	7.65kg A-IX-2	1980s Soviet hollow-base extended-range HE shell. Compatible with 4Zh61 long-range charges. 24.7km max range. Rated for *Msta* only.
3OF61 *Alagez*/3OF64 *Khrebet*-M	42.9/ 43.6	7.8kg A-IX-2	Russian HE shell with different tail sections screwed on: BB gas generator for *Alagez*, hollow-base ring for *Khrebet*-M. Compatible with 4Zh61 long-range charges. 24.4/29km max range. Rated for *Msta* only.
3O23 *Nastoyanie*	42.8	40 x KOBE	Russian cluster munitions shell. KOBE – *kumulativno-oskolochniy boevoy element* ('shaped-charge-fragmentation submunition', similar to US DPICM; 0.042kg explosive). 21km max range. Rated for *Msta* only.
3OF29 *Bekas*	46	6.42kg A-IX-2	1970s Soviet HE shell. *Giatsint* only.
3OF30 *Baklan*	44.8	4.88kg A-IX-2	1970s Soviet HE RAP. 33km max range. *Giatsint* only.
OFdDV	43.5	8kg TNT	Czech HE BB shell. Used with P740 charge as DN1CZ round. Max range: 25.5km. Intended for *Dana*.

203mm

Used exclusively by *Pion* in Ukraine. Ammunition is separate-loading using bagged charges. The US no longer uses 203mm howitzers, but has shipped this ammunition to Ukraine for their *Pions*. Russia has similarly obtained 203mm US ammunition from Iran, which had bought US 203mm howitzers before the 1979 revolution.

Table 5: 203mm Artillery Ammunition Characteristics

Name	Weight (kg)	Filler/Payload	Notes
3OF43 *Albatros*	110	17.8kg A-IX-2	1970s Soviet HE shell.
3OF44 *Burevestnik*-2	102	13.3 A-IX-2	1970s Soviet HE RAP. 47.5km max range.
3O14 *Sklad*	110	24 x 3O16	1980s Soviet cluster munitions shell. Each 3O18 fragmentation submunition contains 0.23kg A-IX-2. 30.4km max range.
HE M106	90	16.4kg TNT/ 17.6 Comp. B	US HE shell. Originally intended for M110 and M115 howitzers but adapted to Soviet 203mm 2A44 gun in Ukraine.
G-620	100	15.4kg TNT	Second World War Soviet concrete-piercing shell. Originally designed for B-4/B-4M howitzers.

240mm

Used exclusively by *Tyulpan* and M-240 mortars in Ukraine.

Table 6: 240mm Mortar Ammunition Characteristics

Name	Weight (kg)	Filler/Payload	Notes
F-864	131	32kg TNT	Soviet fin-stabilised HE mortar bomb. Main charge within projectile tail with bagged charges tied to tail as needed.
3F2 *Gagara*	228	46.5kg TGAF-5M	Soviet fin-stabilised HE rocket-assisted mortar bomb. 20km max range.
3F5 *Smelchak*	134	21.4kg A-IX-2	Soviet laser-guided fin-stabilised HE mortar bomb with pulse rockets for trajectory correction. Part of *Smelchak* (1K113) PGM complex. 9.2km max range.
3O8 *Nerpa*	227	14 x 3O10	Soviet fin-stabilised cluster munitions rocket-assisted mortar bomb. Each 3O10 fragmentation submunition contains 0.64kg A-IX-2. 19.3km max range.

APPENDIX 2: AMMUNITION PREPARATION TIMES

The following is a table for the time standards (in man-hours) to prepare 1,000 rounds of ammunition for combat use, as adapted from the textbook *Rukovodstvo po ekspluatatsii raketno-artilleriyskogo vooruzheniya*, published by the MORF in 2006.

The time standard includes the time to take the 1,000 shells and the fuse out of their crates and screw them together, carrying time included, as well as to prepare propellant charges prior to being issued to the unit. In modern practice, this is more usually done at the combat position itself. However, the author believes that this table provides a useful frame of reference in the logistical effort required to support these pieces with ammunition.

Table 7: Ammunition Preparation Times

Artillery Piece	Time Standard (Man-hours)
100mm T-12/MT-12 *Rapira*	169
120mm mortar	240
122mm D-30/2S1 *Gvozdika*	150
130mm M-46	191
152mm ML-20/D-20/2S3 *Akatsiya*/2A65 *Msta-B*/2S19 *Msta-S*	247
152mm 2A36 *Giatsint-B*/2S5 *Giatsint-S*	265
203mm 2S7 *Pion*	1,050
240mm M-240/2S4 *Tyulpan*	720

APPENDIX 3: BARREL LIFE

The following is a table for the barrel life of various artillery pieces described in the book. Most data is taken from the textbook *Rukovodstvo po ekspluatatsii raketno-artilleriyskogo vooruzheniya*, published by the MORF in 2006, except where noted.

Barrel life is usually measured in terms of the number of effective full charge rounds fired from the gun before barrel wear results in a pre-specified drop in the muzzle velocity (usually 10 percent, though it was not given in the textbook), after which the barrel should be replaced. They are only provided as a frame of reference to illustrate how barrel life decreases inversely with the performance of the ammunition (i.e. muzzle velocity/kinetic energy), and one should directly compare these figures with Western ones without knowing the exact standards used.

A gun may be fired past this barrel life, but this will result in a loss of accuracy and, if the barrel is worn down enough, the barrel may burst and possibly prematurely detonate the shell with potentially lethal consequences for the crew.

Table 8: Artillery Barrel Life

Artillery Piece	Barrel Life (Rounds)
122mm D-30/2S1 *Gvozdika*	2,500–6,000
122mm D-74	1,700
130mm M-46	1,100–1,200
152mm D-20/2S3 *Akatsiya*	3,500
152mm 2A36 *Giatsint*-B/2S5 *Giatsint*-S	1,000–1,200
152mm 2A65 *Msta*-B/2S19 *Msta*-S	2,000 (long-range); 4,000 (regular)*
203mm 2S7 *Pion*	400–450

* From 2S19 TO; lower figure is for 4Zh61 long-range 'super' charge.

SELECTED BIBLIOGRAPHY

Military Manuals/Textbooks/Manufacturer Brochures

For the maintenance/operation of equipment, the Soviets, Russians, and Ukrainians issued technical descriptions (*tekhnicheskoe opisanie*, TO), user manuals (*instruktsiya po ekspluatatsii*, IE, *rukovodstvo sluzhby*, RS, or *rukovodstvo po ekspluatatsii*, RE) and military repair manuals (*rukovodstvo po voennomu/voyskovomu remontu*, RVR). Often, the TO and IE were combined into one book (TOIE). Firing tables (*tablitsy strelby*, TS) and catalogues of parts (*katalog detaley*, KD) were also issued. The date is not always printed in these manuals.

All Soviet manuals in Russian unless otherwise noted.

Rukovodstvo po ekspluatatsii raketno-artilleriyskogo vooruzheniya, MORF (2006)

D-20/*Akatsiya*

D-74 & D-20 RS (1958)
D-20 TS (TS No. 271)
D-20 RS (1981)
2S3M(1) TOIE, in four books (2S3M(1).TO1/2/3/4)
2S3M1 TO (*elektroskhema*)

D-30/*Gvozdika*

D-30 TOIE
D-30A TO
D-30 TS (TS No. 145)
2A31 TOIE
2S1 TO (2S1.00.01.TO)
2S1 *Formular* (2S1.00.01.FO)
Universalnoe gusenichnoe legkoe shassi TOIE (2S1.08.001.TO)

Tyulpan

2S4 KD (2S4.KD)
2B8 KD (2B8.2S4.KD1)
M-240 RS (1956)

Giatsint

2A36 TO
2A36/2S5 TOIE (ammunition only; 2A36.TO1/2S5.TO2)
'*Konstruktsiya, ekspluatatsiya, i osnovy proektirovaniya artilleriyskikh orudiy i boepripasov ch.3: samokhodnye artilleriyskie orudiya*' (2S5 textbook)

Pion

Panc.-Sam. 514/85: '*Podwozie Gąsienicowe 2S7*' (Polish translation of Soviet 2S7 chassis TOIE)
2A44 TO Book 1 (2A44.TO)

Nona

2S9 TO
2A51 TO
BTR-D TO

Msta

2A65 TOIE in three books (2A65.TO/TO1/TO2)
2S19 TOIE Book 1 (2S19.TO)
2S19 *pamyatka raschetu* (Ukrainian 'crew memo' based on 2006 Russian manual)

Books

Latukhin, A., '*Bog voyny*', Moskva (1979)
Shirokorad, A., '*Entsiklopediya otechestvennoi artillerii*', Kharvest (2000) [Russian]
Shirokorad, A., '*Otechestvennye minomyoty i reaktivnaya artilleriya*' Kharvest (2000) [Russian]
Bobkov, A., & Ustyantsev, S., '*Boevye mashiny Uraltransmasha kn.3: Uralskiy buket 1966–1988*', Uraltransmash (2023) [Russian]
Sorokin, A., '*Sovetskaya gaubitsa D-30*', Yauza-Eksmo (2018) [Russian]
Baryatinskiy, M., '*Samokhodnye artilleriyskie ustanokvi "Gvozdika", "Pion" i "Msta"*', Bronekollektsiya (2018) [Russian]
Baryatinskiy, M., '*Samokhodnye artilleriyskie ustanovki "Akatsiya", "Tyulpan" i "Giatsint"*', Bronekollektsiya (2017) [Russian]
Fedoseev, S., '*Universalnoe orudie "Nona"*', Yauza-Eksmo (2021) [Russian]
Manson, M., '*Guns, Mortars and Rockets*', Brassey's (1997)
Geneva International Centre for Humanitarian Demining, '*Explosive Ordnance Guide for Ukraine*' (2022)

Periodicals

Tekhnika i Vooruzhenie (TiV) [Russian]
Nowa Tekhnika Wojskowa (NTW) [Polish]

Online Resources

British Artillery of World War 2 (britishartillery.co.uk): extensive resource by Nigel Evans on artillery techniques and technology, mostly covering the Second World War, but also the Cold War and beyond from British perspective.
Boepripasnik (soviet-ammo.ucoz.ru) [Russian]: extensive Russian database on Soviet and Russian artillery ammunition.

ENDNOTES

Introduction

1 V. Kyrey, *'Artilleriya ataka i oborony. Vivod iz primeneniya artillerii na russkom fronte v 1914–1917 gg.'*, Gosvoenizdat (1926), p.75.
2 Latukhin, A., *'Bog voyny'* (1979), p.102.
3 O. Syrota, *'Why is it so important to fire at higher angles?'*, Ammunition 155 mm: en.bk155.com.ua/ефективність-стрільби/
4 St. Petersburg Artillery Museum, *'The History of Russian Artillery since the mid 19th century up to 1917'* (2022): artillery-museum.spb.ru/en/main-exposition/the-history-of-russian-artillery-since-the-mid19th-century-up-to-1917.html
5 For more details from a Soviet perspective, see: V. Lebedev, *'Sparovchik ofitsera nazemnoy artillerii'* (1984).
6 PAB – *Periskopicheskaya artilleriyskaya bussol* (lit. 'periscopic artillery compass').
7 R. Romaniuk, *'Persha bytva "Bohdany". Yak ukrayins'ka SAU prymusyla rosiyan do "zhestu dobroyi voli" na Zmiyinomu'*, Ukrayinska Pravda (2023): pravda.com.ua/articles/2023/02/13/7388834/
8 For reasons unknown to the author, Grau & Bartles call it 'Kharkov' in their publications. The author has not seen this name used in Russian, Soviet, or Ukrainian publications.
9 A. Bobkov and S. Ustyantsev, *'Boevye mashiny Uraltransmasha kn.3: Uralskiy buket 1966–1988'* (2023), p.114–116.
10 J. Watling, and N. Reynolds, *'Meatgrinder: Russian Tactics in the Second Year of its Invasion of Ukraine'*, RUSI (2023).
11 Logika, *'Tactical unit combat control system "Kropyva"'* (2024): logika.ua/en/automation-systems/
12 SVP 7-(07)256, pp.114–125.'

Chapter 1

1 C. Bellamy, *'Red God of War'*, p.3.
2 The author recommends Sasho Todorov's presentation *'The Red God of War?'* on the WW2TV YouTube channel for an introduction to this subject.
3 T. Andreeva and S. Dobrynina, *'Uralskiy konstruktor rasskazal, kak proshla gaubitsa "Akatsiya"'*, RG.ru (2014): rg.ru/2014/08/13/reg-urfo/konstruktor.html
4 S. Belousov, *'Vozrozhdeni, chtob tsely delat pilyu'*, Redstar.ru (2011): old.redstar.ru/2011/03/02_03/2_03.html
5 Andreeva & Dobrynina (2014).
6 SIPRI Fact Sheet 1992, *'Post Cold War Security in and for Europe'* (1992), p.8.
7 *'The Military Balance 1991-92'*, International Institute for Strategic Studies (1991), p.37.
8 *'Dupleks'* and *'tripleks'* are general terms the Soviets often used for describing two or three systems, respectively, that share a common basis.
9 For insight into modern Russian artillery manufacturing, which is still undertaken by these factories leftover from the USSR, the author recommends the Royal United Services Institute (RUSI) and Open Source Centre's 2024 report *'Ore to Ordnance: Disrupting Russia's Artillery Supply Chains'*: rusi.org/explore-our-research/publications/external-publications/ore-ordnance-disrupting-russias-artillery-supply-chains

Chapter 2

1 The original 1931 A-19 had its own carriage before it was unified with the ML-20 in 1937.
2 A. Shirokorad, *'Entsiklopediya otechestvennoi artillerii'* (2000) pp.653–658.
3 *'Artilleriyskoe snazhenie v Velikoy Otechestvennoy voyne 1941–45 (tom 1)'* (1977), GRAU pp.248–250 & 395–396.
4 A. Sorokin, *'Sovetskaya gaubitsa M-10'* (2020) pp.81–88.
5 A. Sorokin, *'Sovetskaya gaubitsa D-1'* (2021) pp.18–26.
6 Sorokin, *'D-1'* pp.74–77.
7 Sorokin, *'D-1'* pp.119–121.
8 Shirokorad, *'Ents. ot. art.'* p.683.
9 Shirokorad, *'Ents. ot. art.'*, pp.704–705.
10 D-20/74 RS (1958), pp.26–32.
11 A. Sorokin, *'152-mm pushka-gaubitsa D-20 (ch.1)'*, TiV 11 (2016).
12 A. Sorokin, *'152-mm pushka-gaubitsa D-20 (ch.2)'*, TiV 12 (2016).
13 Mil.ru, 'D-74 122 mm field gun crews of the Eastern Grouping of Forces destroy AFU formations retreating from Vuhledar in the South Donetsk direction' (2024): function.mil.ru/news_page/country/more.htm?id=12532100@egNews
14 Sorokin, *'D-20 (ch.1)'*.
15 Sorokin, *'D-20 (ch.1)'*.
16 A. Solyankin, I. Zheltov, and K. Kudryashov, *'Otechestvennie bronirovannie mashiny XX vek 1946–1965'* (2005), pp.513–515.
17 Solyankin, Zheltov, and Kudryashov, pp.521–522.
18 Belousov (2014).
19 Bobkov & Ustyantsev, *'Uralskiy buket'*, pp.22–23.
20 Bobkov & Ustyantsev, p.29.
21 Bobkov & Ustyantsev, pp.47 & 59.
22 Andreeva & Dobrynina (2014).
23 Bobkov & Ustyantsev, *'Uralskiy buket'*, p.72.
24 Bobkov & Ustyantsev, p.106.
25 A. Karpenko, *'Sovremennye samokhodnye artilleriyskie orudiya'* (2009), p.17.
26 Bobkov & Ustyantsev, *'Uralskiy buket'*, pp.114–116.
27 TASS.ru, *'"Uralvagonzavod" postavil Minoborony pervuyu partiyu modernizirovannykh SAU "Akatsiya"'* (2021): tass.ru/armiya-i-opk/11363945
28 MORF, *'Rukovodstvo po boevoy rabote ognevykh podrazdeleniy artillerii'* (2002), p.53.
29 Bobkov & Ustyantsev, *'Uralskiy buket'*, pp.105–106.
30 ParkPatriot.ru, *'Samokhodnaya gaubitsa 2S3 "Akatsiya"'*: parkpatriot.ru/o-parke/tekhnika-parka/akatsiya-samokhodnaya-gaubitsa-2s3/
31 VIF2NE.org, *'Artilleriyskoe proizvodstvo...'* (2018): vif2ne.org/nvk/forum/archive/2839/2839270.htm
32 'Altyn73', *'152-mm samokhodnaya gaubitsa 2S19 "Msta-S" v Vooruzhennykh Silakh Rossiyskoy Federatsii. Versiya 2.0'* (2019): altyn73.livejournal.com/1382776.html
33 OSCE SMM Daily Report (21 June 2020), p.9.
34 Mil.ru, *'Boevaya rabota rascheta orudiya D-20 na Severskom'* (2024): мультимедиа.минобороны.рф/multimedia/video/clips/more.htm?id=23357@morfVideoAudioFile
35 Zhirokhov, M., *'Ukrainskiy arsenal: 152-mm samokhodnaya gaubitsa 2S3 Akatsiya'*, Fraza (2019): fraza.com/analytics/284218-ukrainskij-arsenal-152-mm-samohodnaja-gaubitsa-2s3-akatsija-
36 Zhirokhov, M., *'Ukrainskiy arsenal: 152-mm gaubitsa-pushka D-20'*, Fraza (2018): fraza.com/analytics/270334-ukrainskij-arsenal-152-mm-pushka-gaubitsa-d-20-

Chapter 3

1 A. Sorokin, *'Sovetskaya gaubitsa M-30'* (2017), pp.84–87.
2 A. Sorokin, *'Sovetskaya gaubitsa D-30'* (2018), pp.12–16.
3 Sorokin, *'Sovetskaya gaubitsa D-30'* p.17.
4 Sorokin, *'Sovetskaya gaubitsa D-30'* p.21.
5 Sorokin, *'Sovetskaya gaubitsa D-30'* p.10.
6 Contrary to some Western literature, there is no such thing as 'D-30M': only D-30 and D-30A entered service. There is an improved 2A18M-1 with a semi-automatic loader, but it was not adopted for service. Sorokin, *'D-30'* (2018), p.71.
7 Sorokin, *'D-30'* (2018), p.24.
8 Bellamy, *'Red God of War'*, p.122.
9 Bellamy, *'Red God of War'*, pp.26–27.
10 Lviv Media, *'Artillery sniper rifle. How Ukrainian D-30 howitzers work'*, YouTube (2022): youtube.com/watch?v=s6IgE9Wj89w
11 NTV, *'Voennoe Delo – D-30 122mm howitzer'*, YouTube (2003): youtu.be/e1AiBLK4uHc
12 Sorokin, *'D-30'* (2018), pp.26–27.
13 Sorokin, *'D-30'* (2018), p.30.
14 Bobkov & Ustyantsev, *'Uralskiy buket'*, p.18.
15 NPO Strela, *'Mobilnaya RLS nazemnoy artilleriyskoy razvedki SNAR-10'* (2011): npostrela.com/ru/products/museum/82/209/

16 M. Baryatinskiy, '*Samokhodnye artilleriyskie ustanokvi "Gvozdika", "Pion" i "Msta"*' (2018), p.3.
17 M. Knyazev, '*2S1 Gvozdika*', *Russkie Tank* No. 32 (2011), p.5.
18 D. Sobczak, '*The TOPAZ Artillery Modernisation Programme*', Military Technology 28-5, (2004) p.84.
19 T. Szulc, '*Morski Goździk – polska wersja samobieżnej haubicy 2S1*', NTW 335 (2019), pp.92–98.
20 Bobkov & Ustyantsev, '*Uralskiy buket*', p.18.
21 K. Ryabov, '*Self-propelled guns 2S34 "Khosta" participate in the Special Operation*', Topwar.ru (19 Feb 2023): en.topwar.ru/211194-samohodnye-orudija-2s34-hosta-uchastvujut-v-specoperacii.html
22 Baryatinskiy, '*Gvozdika, Pion i Msta*', p.9.
23 GVTM.ru, '*Samokhodnaya gaubitsa Gvozdika 2S1 122-mm*', (2010): old.gvtm.ru/samohodnaya_gaubica_gvozdika_2s1
24 Knyazev, '*Gvozdika*', p.9.
25 R. Then, '*2S1 Gvozdika*', Tankograd blog.
26 Sorokin, '*D-30*' (2018), p.24.
27 Baryatinskiy, '*Gvozdika, Pion i Msta*', pp.2–3.
28 A. Mikhaylov, '*Minoborony otkazalos ot legendarnoy gaubitsy D-30*', Izvestia (2013): izvestia.ru/news/545693
29 M. Zhirokhov, '*SAU 2S1 "Hvozdika" ZSU v khodi viyini na Donbasi (2014–2015)*', Ukrainian Military Pages (2016): ukrmilitary.com/2016/01/2s1-gvozdika-in-donbas-war.html
30 Narodna Armiia, '*Hvozdiku modernizuyut u Kharkovi*' (11 Feb 2016): na.mil.gov.ua/29684-gvozdiku-modernizuyut-u-xarkovi
31 Defense Express, '*V Ukrayini stvoreniy pershiy vitchiznyaniy stvol dlya gaubitsi D-30 (foto)*' (2020): defence-ua.com/news/v_ukrajini_stvorenij_pershij_vitchiznjanij_stvol_dlja_gaubitsi_d_30_foto-397.html
32 M. Zhirokhov, '*Ukrainskiy arsenal: gaubitsy D-30*', Fraza (2017): fraza.com/analytics/259020-ukrainskij-arsenal-gaubitsy-d-30-
33 For significantly more historical background and specific technical details of the T-12/MT-12 and other Cold War Soviet towed AT guns, the author recommends Ryan Then's Tankograd blog article: thesovietarmourblog.blogspot.com/2020/12/soviet-towed-anti-tank-guns.html
34 M. Zhirokhov, '*Mnogotselevaya "Rapira". Artilleristy VSU gotovyat novyye instrumenty dlya umershchvleniya "gibridov"*', dsnews.ua (2018): dsnews.ua/politics/mnogotselevaya-rapira-artilleristy-vsu-gotovyat-novye-instrumenty-27072018080000
35 M. Moss, 'Ukraine's New & Improved Home Made Self-Propelled Gun', The Armourer's Bench (2022): armourersbench.com/2022/10/09/ukraines-new-improved-home-made-self-propelled-gun/
36 P. Koltsov, '*Zamkomvzvoda zayavil, chto MT-12 «razbirayet na raz» osnovaniye VSU.*' Zvezda (2024): pablic.tvzvezda.ru/news/2024851251-VZqaT.html

Chapter 4

1 M. Manson, '*Guns, Mortars and Rockets*' (1997), pp.27–29.
2 A. Losik and K. Cherentsova, '*Creation of Soviet mortars in mid-1930s: searches and design solutions*', *Voenno-Istoricheskiy Zhurnal* No. 9 (2018), pp.39–43.
3 A. Isaev, '*V prodolzhenie temy raskhoda boepripasov*', VIF2NE.org (2009): vif2ne.org/nvk/forum/2/archive/1706/1706490.htm
4 A. Shirokorad, '*Otechestvennye minomyoty i reaktivnaya artilleriya*' (2000), p.119.
5 '*Ot. min.*' (2000), pp.124, 191.
6 Later Yurginskiy Mashzavod; declared bankrupt and liquidated in 2020. '*LLC "Yurginsky mashzavod"*': basis.myseldon.com/en/company/1054230016180
7 M-240 RS (1956), p.6.
8 In the early stages, it was also called 'M240-S'.
9 Bobkov & Ustyantsev, '*Uralskiy buket*', pp.24–28.
10 Bobkov & Ustyantsev, pp.59–61.
11 S. Suvorov, '*Tsvety dlya elitnykh klumb (ch.2)*', TiV 1 (2019), pp.2–13. Shirokorad, '*Ot. min.*' (2000), p.196 gives ₽30,500 for *Akatsiya* instead.
12 VIF2NE.org, '*Art. pro.*' (2018). Motovilikha claims to have produced 588 2B8s; presumably some of these would have been kept as spares.
13 Shirokorad, '*Ot. min.*' (2000), p.204.
14 Baryatinskiy, M., '*Samokhodnye artilleriyskie ustanovki "Akatsiya", "Tyulpan" i "Giatsint"*' (2017), p.42.
15 Suvorov, TiV 1 (2019), pp.2–13.
16 S. Valchenko and A. Ramm, '*"Tyulpan" vyidet v onlain*', Izvestia (2018): iz.ru/696810/sergei-valchenko-aleksei-ramm/tiulpan-vyidet-v-onlain
17 Mil.ru, '*Units of the Russian Defence Ministry receive 2S4 Tulpan modernized self-propelled mortars*' (13 Nov 2017): eng.mil.ru/en/news_page/country/more.htm?id=12150585@egNews
18 Bobkov & Ustyantsev, '*Uralskiy buket*', pp.105–106.
19 Ballistic Research Laboratories, '*Ballistic and Engineering Data for Shell, HE, 240-mm, M114 with Fuzes, PD, M51A4; MT, M67A3; and CP, M78*', Ballistic Research Laboratories Handbook of Ballistic and Engineering Data for Ammunition No. 240-1-114 (1949), p.23.
20 Suvorov, TiV 1 (2019), pp.2–13.
21 Suvorov, TiV 1 (2019), pp.2–13.
22 Izvestia, '*Artilleriya narashchivaet moshch*' (2017): iz.ru/675176/evgenii-andreev-bogdan-stepovoi-aleksei-ramm/artilleriia-narashchivaet-moshch
23 Focus.ua, '*"Skladyvali" podezdy: propagandist priznal chto VS RF razrushali mnogoetazhki Mariupolya (foto)*' (21 Mar 2023): focus.ua/voennye-novosti/556096-skladyvali-podezdy-propagandist-priznal-chto-vs-rf-razrushali-mnogoetazhki-mariupolya-foto

Chapter 5

1 M-46/47 RS pt. 1 (1981), p.4.
2 A. Shirokorad, '*Atomniy taran XX veka*' (2005), pp.178–179.
3 D. Smith, '*175mm M113 Cannon: Historical Perspective on the Cannon that changed our Cannon Design Process*', NDIA Joint Armaments Symposium (2012).
4 TM 9-2300-216-10 C6, pp.2-95–2-100.
5 Bobkov & Ustyantsev, '*Uralskiy buket*', pp.73–74.
6 Bobkov & Ustyantsev, '*Uralskiy buket*', pp.74–86.
7 Baryatinskiy, '*Akatsiya, Tyulpan i Giatsint*' (2017), pp.55–56.
8 Militarnyi, '*Ukrainian Defence Forces are using Finnish Giatsint-B field guns*' (2023): mil.in.ua/en/news/ukrainian-defence-forces-are-using-finnish-giatsint-b-field-guns/
9 VIF2NE.org, '*Art. pro.*' (2018).
10 Bobkov & Ustyantsev, '*Uralskiy buket*', pp.106, 114, 116.
11 A. Derevyanchuk, O. Kravchuk, A. Vakal, and S. Nikul, '*Sposib vymiru dovzhyny zaryadnoyi kamori stvoliv*', Viyskova akademiya (m. Odesa), Zbirnyk naukovykh prats No. 1 Vol. 9 (2018).
12 InformNapalm, '*Russian Giatsint-B artillery and Ural-632301 detected by aerial recon in Donbas*' (2016): informnapalm.org/en/russian-artillery-detected-aerial-recon-donbas/
13 M. Zhirokhov, '*Ukrainskiy arsenal: 152-mm samohodnaya pushka 2S5 Giatsint-S*', Fraza (2020): fraza.com/analytics/288167-ukrainskij-arsenal-152-mm-samohodnaja-pushka-2s5-giatsint-s-
14 ArmyTV, '*Rosiany pomyraiut vid trofeiynoyi SAU*', YouTube (2024): youtu.be/gII-eahdML8
15 'Kloch4', '*Tsvetochek gennatsbalya*', LiveJournal (2015): kloch4.livejournal.com/4113.html
16 Militarnyi, '*Bohdana-B: prospects of towed artillery for the Armed Forces of Ukraine*' (023): mil.in.ua/en/articles/bohdana-b-prospects-of-towed-artillery-for-the-armed-forces-of-ukraine/

Chapter 6

1 TM 43-0001-28, pp.3-175–3-176.
2 US Army Artillery and Missile School, '*Artillery Trends*' (1966), p.13.
3 Placard at the Moscow Museum of the Great Patriotic War: commons.wikimedia.org/wiki/File:203_mm_B-4M_howitzer_in_the_Great_Patriotic_War_Museum_5-jun-2014_01.jpg
4 Production would later resume at Barrikady, but mostly for export to Syria and Egypt in response to Israeli M107s. 12 more were built by 1971.
5 Shirokorad, '*Ents. ot. art.*' pp.778–781.
6 A. Efremov, and B. Spiridonov, '*SAU povyshennogo mogushchestva*' (pt. 1), TiV 12 (2012), pp.2–8.
7 Shirokorad, '*Atomniy taran*', pp.184–187.
8 Bobkov & Ustyantsev, '*Uralskiy buket*', p.73.
9 S. Kudryavtsev, '*U istokov sozdaniya pushki "Pion"*', Za inzhenernye kadry No. 1 (2017).
10 Shirokorad, '*Atomniy taran*', pp.184–187.
11 N. Popov, V. Petrov, A. Popov, and M. Ashik, '*Bez tayn i sekretov*' (1995), pp.272–278.

12 A. Yefremov, '"*Pion" – sed'moy «tsvetok» v artilleriyskom «bukete» i yego unifitsirovannyye nasledniki*', Otvaga2004 (24 Aug 2013): otvaga2004.ru/tiv/pion-sedmoj-cvetok/
13 S. Suvorov, '*Tsvety dlya elitnykh klumb (ch.3)*', TiV 2 (2019), pp.7–18.
14 A. Efremov, and B. Spiridonov, '*SAU povyshennogo mogushchestva*' (pt. 2), TiV 1 (2013), pp.18–29. Likely named after the river Malka.
15 Suvorov, TiV 2 (2019), pp.7–18.
16 Derevyanchuk et al. (2018).
17 Derevyanchuk et al. (2018).
18 Efremov & Spiridonov, TiV 1 (2013), pp.18–29.
19 Efremov & Spiridonov, TiV 1 (2013), pp.18–29.
20 Suvorov, TiV 2 (2019), pp.7–18.
21 Efremov & Spiridonov, TiV 1 (2013), pp.18–29.
22 Bobkov & Ustyantsev, '*Uralskiy buket*', pp.105–106.
23 Kudryavtsev, Za inzh. kad. 1 (2017).
24 Yefremov, Otvaga2004 (2013).
25 A. Karpenko, '*Sovremennye smokhodnye artilleriyskie orudiya*' (2009), pp.36–41.
26 Yefremov, Otvaga2004 (2013).
27 Efremov & Spiridonov, TiV 12 (2012), pp.2–8.
28 Efremov & Spiridonov, TiV 1 (2013), pp.18–29.
29 Ukrainska Pravda, '*Treba bulo bachyty, yak "Piony" vahoyu 47 tonn svoyim khodom rukhalysya po prospektu Peremohy – kombryh 43 bryhady Oleh Shevchuk*' (2023): pravda.com.ua/articles/2023/02/22/7390363/
30 Shirokorad, '*Atomniy taran*', pp.184–187.
31 Izvestia, '*Artilleriya narashchivaet moshch*' (2017): iz.ru/675176/evgenii-andreev-bogdan-stepovoi-aleksei-ramm/artilleriia-narashchivaet-moshch
32 M. Zhirokhov, and A. Kikavskiy, '*Potuzhnyi argument dlia okupanta*' (2023), pp.27–41.
33 Ukrainska Pravda, '*Treba bulo bachyty*' (2023).
34 Militarnyi, '*Ukrainian 2S7 Pion shoots with American 203mm rounds*' (2023): mil.in.ua/en/news/ukrainian-2s7-pion-shoots-with-american-203mm-rounds/
35 Essanews, 'Iran supplies American shells for Russian use in Soviet-Era artillery' (2024): essanews.com/iran-supplies-american-shells-for-russian-use-in-soviet-era-artillery,7019602691844225a
36 SPKh Vodogray, '*Intervyu z Andriyem Kobzarem — dosvidchenim artileristom i komandirom rozrakhunku Panzerhaubitze 2000*', Drukarnia (2023): drukarnia.com.ua/articles/intervyu-z-andriyem-kobzarem-dosvidchenim-artileristom-i-komandirom-rozrakhunku-panzerhaubitze-2000-OULoB
37 A. Kharuk, '*Navishcho rashtsi "Koksany"?*' (2025): atez72.blogspot.com/2025/02/blog-post.html?m=1
38 J. Zhang, and D. Fu, '*Zhǔtǐ sīxiǎng de wēilì jiēmì cháoxiǎn Gǔshān dàpào*', Ordnance Knowledge No. 12 (2015).
39 J. Kim, '*North Korea has sent over 13K containers of weapons to Russia, Seoul says*', NK News (2024): nknews.org/2024/08/north-korea-has-sent-over-13k-containers-of-weapons-to-russia-seoul-says/
40 J. Bermudez, Jr., '*M-1978 and M-1979 170 mm Self-propelled Guns, Part I*', KPA Journal Vol. 2 No. 6 (2011).
41 J. Bermudez, Jr., '*M-1978 and M-1979 170 mm Self-propelled Guns, Part II*', KPA Journal Vol. 2 No. 7 (2011).
42 See photo by Stefan Krasowski: upload.wikimedia.org/wikipedia/commons/d/dc/170mm_M1989_Koksan_-_North_Korea_Victory_Day-2013_03.jpg
43 Bermudez, KPA Journal Vol. 2 No. 6 (2011).
44 Zhang & Fu, Ordnance Knowledge No. 12 (2015).
45 Gamersky, '*Jiǎng wǔ táng: Jiǎrú zhànzhēng míngtiān bàofā cháoxiǎn jiāng yòng zhèxiē yíngzhàn měiguó!*' (2016): wap.gamersky.com/news/content-758060_2.html
46 R. Francona, '*North Korean M1978 Koksan Gun – the Iranian angle*', LinkedIn (2017): linkedin.com/pulse/north-korean-m1978-koksan-gun-iranian-angle-rick-francona
47 Zhang & Fu, Ordnance Knowledge No. 12 (2015).
48 Mike Fredenburg used ballistics simulation software with the M107 as a reference to evaluate the likely trade-offs the 170mm gun needed to achieve the credited ranges; take these figures with a pinch of salt. See: M. Fredenburg, '*The 170 mm Koksan, North Korea's Not-So-Frightening Tool of Terror*', National Review (2018): nationalreview.com/2018/04/north-korean-artillery-koksan-gun-could-be-inaccurate-unreliable/
49 H. Tarakh, '*Npavitzer 170 milimetri M1978 Koksan*', Jangaavaran (): jangaavaran.ir/29559-2/
50 For more details, see: E. Hooton, T. Cooper, and F. Nadimi, '*The Iran–Iraq War Vol. 3: Iraq's Triumph*' (2017), pp.3, 43, 49, 77.
51 Militarnyi, '*North Korean M1989 Koksan long-range artillery systems spotted in Russia*' (2024): mil.in.ua/en/news/north-korean-m1989-koksan-long-range-artillery-systems-spotted-in-russia/
52 C. Miller, and I. Koshiw, '*North Korean casualties in Storm Shadow strike on Kursk, says Kyiv*', Financial Times (2024): ft.com/content/b6fa9001-632e-449e-9c4f-e74d404e709e

Chapter 7

1 A motorised towed gun such as the SD-57 and SD-44 is referred to as a '*samodvizushchayasya pushka*' in Russian, as opposed to a conventional SPG like the *Akatsiya* ('*samokhodnaya pushka*'). Both can be translated as 'self-propelled guns' but for clarity, the former will not be referred to as such.
2 S. Fedoseev, '*Universalnoe orudie "Nona"*' (2021), pp.7–13.
3 Fedoseev, '*Nona*', pp.10–13.
4 *Obus explosif en fonte malléable perlitique de 120 mm, prérayé modèle* F1 — '120 mm HE shell in pearlitic malleable cast iron, pre-rifled, model F1'
5 PAD – *propulsion additionnelle.*
6 Marest, M., and Tauzin, M., '*COMHART Tome 9: Armement de gros calibre*' (2008), p.230.
7 Fedoseev, '*Nona*', p.17.
8 Fedoseev, '*Nona*', pp.19–24.
9 Fedoseev, '*Nona*', pp.25–32.
10 V. Kadochnikov, '*Motovilikha. Prodolzhenie legendy*' (2011), p.156.
11 A. Shirokorad, '*Arsenal: Novoe oruzhie nazemnoy artillerii*', Bratishka (2011): bratishka.ru/archiv/2011/8/2011_8_12.php
12 Fedoseev, '*Nona*', pp.92–96.
13 Fedoseev, '*Nona*', pp.102–104.
14 Mil.ru, '*Gornye motostrelki TsVO poluchili na vooruzhenie samokhodnye orudiya "Nona-SVK"*' (2018): function.mil.ru/news_page/country/more.htm?id=12157987@egNews
15 Fedoseev, '*Nona*', p.106.
16 According to common legend, because a highly respected commander stated that his wife's name was Nona and that she was not a 'B' (*blyad* – 'whore'). Fedoseev, '*Nona*', p.99.
17 Fedoseev, '*Nona*', p.106.
18 VIF2NE.org, '*Art. pro.*' (2018).
19 Fedoseev, '*Nona*', p.128.
20 Fedoseev, '*Nona*', p.57.
21 Fedoseev, '*Nona*', pp.67–68.
22 Fedoseev, '*Nona*', p.95.
23 Fedoseev, '*Nona*', p.65.
24 Fedoseev, '*Nona*', pp.34–35.
25 For more information about *Vena*, *Lotos*, *Floks*, etc., see Fedoseev, '*Nona*', pp.149–162.
26 Fedoseev, '*Nona*', p.95.
27 M. Zhirokhov, '*Ukrainskiy arsenal: 120-mm samokhodnaya pushka-minomyot 2S9 Nona-S*', Fraza (2018): fraza.com/analytics/265805-ukrainskij-arsenal-120-mm-samohodnaja-pushka-minomet-2s9-nona-s
28 Defense Express, '*Ukrainian Version of the Nona Self-Propelled Mortar On the BMP Chassis Went Into Series (Video)*' (2023): en.defence-ua.com/industries/ukrainian_version_of_the_nona_self_propelled_mortar_on_the_bmp_chassis_went_into_series_video-6004.html
29 For more information about *Rak*, the author recommends Defence24's article: defence24.pl/sily-zbrojne/mozdzierz-samobiezny-rak-kalibru-120-mm

Chapter 8

1 Russian TV programme '*Voennoe Delo*' episode on the *Msta*-B notes that '*msta*' is also an archaic Russian word for 'revenge'.
2 P. Kebalo, Ya. Mormilo, I. Radenko, S. Solovey, and D. Ugnenko, '*Bazoviy tip khodovoy chasti dlya perspektivnogo tanka*', Integrirovannie tekhnologii i energosberezhenie (2007) 3, p.105.
3 O. Zheltonozhko and V. Belogrud, '*Msta po-Uralski. Borba na samokhodnuyu artilleriyu*', Otvaga2004 (2013): otvaga2004.ru/kaleydoskop/kaleydoskop-art/msta-po-uralski/

4 2S19 TO, p.139.
5 BMPD, *'Proizvodstvo i modernizatsiya 152-mm samokhodnykh orudiy na "Uraltransmashe"'*, LiveJournal (2015): bmpd.livejournal.com/1247401.html
6 Bobkov & Ustyantsev, *'Uralskiy buket'*, pp.114–116.
7 2S19 TO, p.139.
8 ChTZ, *'Partiya "Msta-S" s dvigatelyami ChTZ otpravlena Minoborony RF'* (2021): chtz.ru/news/3183/
9 Bastion-Karpenko, *'International military-technical forum Army-2015. News'* (2016): bastion-karpenko.ru/armia-2015-news-10/
10 Zheltonozhko & Belogrud, *'Msta po-Uralski'*.
11 Zheltonozhko & Belogrud, *'Msta po-Uralski'*.
12 'Altyn73', *'152-mm samokhodnaya gaubitsa 2S19 "Msta-S" v Vooruzhennykh Silakh Rossiyskoy Federatsii. Versiya 2.0'*, LiveJournal (2019): altyn73.livejournal.com/1382776.html
13 T. Cooper, *'Ukraine War: Q & A, 24 July 2022'*, Medium (2022): medium.com/@x_TomCooper_x/ukraine-war-q-a-24-july-2022-fbaa25166f0e
14 M. Zhirokhov, *'SAU Msta-S v boyu'* (2019), pp.13–14.
15 V. Siverskyi, *'152-mm haubytsi «Msta-B» v ZS Ukrayiny'*, Ukrainian Military Pages (2015): ukrmilitary.com/2015/12/msta-b-afu.html
16 Dobrik live, *'Rare Howitzer 'COW'. Features of russian SPA 2S19 'Msta-S' 152 mm. On Combat Duty'*, YouTube (2024): youtu.be/625KpLP1a7s
17 This is claimed on the Russian Wikipedia article on *Koalitsiya*-SV, citing Belyanskaya, O., *'40 let na strazhe otechestva i mira.'* (2010), pp.85–87, a limited circulation book published by Burevestnik themselves.
18 A. Khlopotov, *'Nachato proizvodstvo SAU 2S35 "Koalitsiya-SV"'*, Blogspot (2014): gurkhan.blogspot.com/2014/02/235.html
19 TASS, *'Rossiyskiye voyska poluchili noveyshiye SAU "Koalitsiya-SV"'* (2024): tass.ru/armiya-i-opk/19677215
20 E. Perov, *'Nasha SAU 2S35 "Koalitsiya-SV" ne mozhet ispol'zovat' boyekomplekt drugikh rossiyskikh samokhodok.'*, TopWar (2023): topwar.ru/214587-prosim-otpravit-v-zonu-specoperacii-sau-koalicija-sv-a-streljat-iz-nee-chem-budem.html
21 In the 1980s, the Soviets had experimented with a wheeled *Msta* variant known as *Msta*-K (GRAU: 2S21) but lost interest, though this concept has been revived in the wheeled variant of *Koalitsiya*-SV known as *Koalitsiya*-SV-KSh (GRAU: 2S35-1), which is still under development.
22 D. Ilyin, *'Artilleriyskaya sistema "Malva" provela pokazatelnyye strelby'*, NaukaTekhnika.com (2021): web.archive.org/web/20230225075812/https://naukatehnika.com/artillerijskaya-sistema-«malva»-provela-pokazatelnyie-strelbyi.html
23 Militarnyi, *'Latest Russian 2S43 Malva SPG Spotted on Battlefield for First Time'* (2024): mil.in.ua/en/news/latest-russian-2s43-malva-spg-spotted-on-battlefield-for-first-time/
24 A. Kharuk, *'Malvotsint? Nova rosiyska SAU'* (2024): atez72.blogspot.com/2024/12/blog-post_27.html
25 VESTI, *'Kadry raboty novogo SAU "Giatsint-K"'*, Vkontakte (2025): vk.com/video-24136539_456365734

ABOUT THE AUTHOR

Wen Jian Chung is a PhD student at the University of California, Irvine with a long-term interest in tank development, particularly Soviet, Russian and Ukrainian tanks. This is his third book for Helion.